And Then
The Phone Rang

And Then
The Phone Rang

What I've Learned about Life,
Love, and Lasagna

KATRINA MUSTO

authorHOUSE®

AuthorHouse™
1663 Liberty Drive
Bloomington, IN 47403
www.authorhouse.com
Phone: 1 (800) 839-8640

Published by AuthorHouse 04/05/2016

ISBN: 978-1-5049-6073-1 (sc)
ISBN: 978-1-5049-6072-4 (hc)
ISBN:978-1-5049-6071-7 (e)

Library of Congress Control Number: 2015918500

Print information available on the last page.

To Ant, Dad, and Poppy; the Musto Men. Thank you for all the life lessons you taught me.

Life

*Some names have been changed.

Growing up, every Sunday night my family gathered at my Granny and Poppy's house across town for spaghetti dinner. If I slept over the night before, I watched Granny roll the meatballs and brown the sausage that Sunday morning before dropping each in the sauce to simmer. I thought every family spent their Sunday nights like that, and I loved our family ritual. After dinner was over, we all retreated into the living room and watched TV. Then we hugged and kissed good-bye and went to our homes to prepare for the school and work week.

Although my time with my family was special and something I looked forward to, school wasn't. Due to being painfully shy, I had trouble fitting in. I was bullied for being overweight and had teachers who didn't care enough to help me in the subjects I struggled in. In between being ridiculed for my size and feeling as if I were dumb, I had very few close friends and was often alone.

I had two great best friends while growing up, and they were my only saving grace. I met Sierra and Rachel in kindergarten, and we were in the same Girl Scouts troop together. We each had younger siblings who were near in age and mothers who were involved in school functions. The two of them lived six houses apart in a suburban neighborhood about five minutes away from the busy street where I lived. Sleepovers, Halloween, and numerous birthday parties with both of them made life better. Sierra and Rachel were like night and day, however, and I fell in the middle, being a little bit of both of them.

I didn't become good friends with Sierra until third grade, when we were placed in the same class. Even back then, she had a wild streak to her. Sierra would tell a joke and get a group to burst into laughter; she was the girl the boys had crushes on, the girl who always had a ton of girls attend her annual birthday sleepover. I was content living life on the sidelines and taking in all the excitement that followed her. While I was socially awkward and not exactly considered a hot tamale, Sierra was. Boys *adored* her.

One particular incident occurred when we were about eight years old. Sierra liked a boy in our class and wanted me to pass him a note from her. The note said, "I like you. Do you like me?" As her loyal sidekick, I, of course, said yes. I put the note on his desk and slipped away. He came over to me and asked who had given him the note. While all eyes and ears were on me, I began to stutter. He asked again, and before I knew it, I said, "Sierra."

She wanted to kill me, as you can imagine. But I didn't fully grasp the whole concept of "Shhh! It's a secret note to my crush. Don't tell him it's from me." I was a buffoon. At least now we laugh about it. That's just how life with Sierra was while growing up. Wherever she went, I followed. Whatever she told me to do, I did (to an extent).

Rachel was the opposite of Sierra. She was quiet, and if someone made her upset, she cried. She and I preferred to stay in and rent teen movies starring Freddie Prinze Jr. while munching on popcorn or my mom's homemade pizza. I became best friends with her in the fourth grade, when she was seated next to me in class. Sierra became placed in another classroom that year, so we saw her on the playground at recess and during Girl Scouts.

Rachel and I started having sleepovers every Friday night, alternating between her house and mine. We didn't have to ask each other; it was simply understood where to be at what time. The Friday nights when she came to my house were fun; she arrived after dinner, and we painted our nails or made ice cream sundaes with my mom and my younger sister, Lin, in the kitchen. Immediately after that, we retreated to my room, closed the door, and put on the latest Backstreet Boys CD and choreographed our own dance moves to it. My favorite member was Nick Carter, and I really and truly believed I would marry him one day. We both liked pizza, the color green, and telling jokes—it was meant to be. So there we were, week after week, dancing and laughing in our sleeping bags until the sun came up.

Since Rachel and I spent so much time together, our teachers quickly caught on. We still hung out with Sierra, but she had made friends with some of the more popular girls in our grade and was doing her own thing. We even went as far as to get a blue heart necklace that was cracked in half; one half said "Best," and the other half said "Friend." We were attached at the hip.

Well, the day came when we were due to find out what class we were going to be in for fifth grade, and one at a time, we walked up to the front of the classroom for our assignment. I came back and asked everyone around me what class he or she was in. I asked one boy who sat near me what teacher he had, and it turned out he was in a different class. I continued to ask all the other boys and girls while I waited for Rachel's turn. I forgot that I had asked that boy, so I asked him again.

He said, "I just told you who I have for fifth grade. Stop asking!" (I made a mental note *not* to have him sign my yearbook.) And then Rachel came back and broke the news; she had been placed in a different classroom. So the recess bell rang, and I cried on the swing set. Sierra tried to comfort me by announcing she was in the same class as me. "But ... it's not the same," I managed to get out while my sobs grew louder. For a person without many friends, that day was heartbreaking. But that was just my first taste of life's unfairness.

Fifth grade arrived, and there I was, talking to my best friend in the bus lineup and then walking into a different class once we entered the building. That September, Sierra and I got invited to a pool party for a girl who went to church and school with us. Sierra kept encouraging me to dive into the pool, and despite my best efforts not to try, she won. While I was a natural fish who spent hours in my own pool, I couldn't dive to save my life. There I was, holding my nose with one hand and plunging into the pool in my navy-blue Winnie the Pooh bathing suit from Kmart.

That was when I noticed it. Two of the popular girls and the birthday girl were snickering and looking my way. I jumped in, with the splashes getting louder each time. I knew I was the biggest girl at that party, so my tasteful one-piece suit stood out. Everyone else wore trendy bikinis, displaying bony, undeveloped bodies. I told Sierra I had no desire to dive again, and when she asked why, I shrugged. She wasn't buying it, so we continued to swim. She asked again what was wrong, and I blurted out, "The girls over there are making fun of you and me." While there was clearly nothing wrong with her, I was too ashamed to say it was me they were targeting.

And just like that, Sierra swam over to the others and blurted out, "Hey! What is your problem?"

The birthday girl gave her an odd look and said, "Nothing. What are you talking about?" Sierra had no intention of stepping down; she was moving full speed ahead as I watched this whole encounter in silence.

She continued, "I saw you looking our way and laughing, so something is funny. What's your problem?" The birthday girl and her two other cronies smirked and insisted they weren't talking about us. I finally told Sierra to forget it. We changed out of our wet bathing suits and got ready for pizza and cake with everyone else. And that was the beginning of our fifth-grade year.

The year 1997 was a whirlwind; the world was changing, and so were we. The rise of boy bands made life a little more exciting, as was the presence of the media phenomenon the Spice Girls. Each girl in my grade had a favorite "Spice" they idolized. I liked Sporty Spice because I could relate to being a tomboy with a ponytail in my hair every day and worshipping black Adidas sweatpants. I thought Posh was gorgeous and so fashionable; I wondered how on earth she walked in such itty-bitty outfits and high heels. I used to close my bedroom door and stare into our backyard as I pretended to be Posh Spice. I imagined the trees were my audience, and I was singing to a sold-out crowd, using Lin's Spice Girl microphone.

I was in the chorus at school, and my dad always told me I had a good voice, so naturally I wanted to be a pop singer. Some days I belted out Madonna songs, and years later it would become Selena or Britney Spears songs; I studied their videos to get their dance moves down pat, even down to Selena's famous hand gestures and Britney's hip gyrations. All this was behind closed doors, of course, because I assumed being overweight with bushy hair and crooked teeth wasn't going to get the notice of any music moguls, so my concerts were always in the privacy of my bedroom.

The Spice Girls were overtly sexual in their music and presence, and my dad wasn't a fan. He didn't like me listening to them or watching them on TV, so I had to sneak it. My mom taped each performance they had on Jay Leno and David Letterman's shows—via a VCR ... Remember those?—and I watched them the next day after school. I remember getting a Toys "R" Us gift card for my birthday that year, and when my mom took me to pick something out, I chose *Spice World*, the Spice Girls movie. My dad saw it on the counter when I got home, and I overheard him say to my mom, "If I would have known she was going to pick this out with her gift card, I would have taken it away."

When Sierra's birthday rolled around that April, she announced she was having a Spice Girls sleepover, complete with our dressing up as our favorite band member. I choose Sporty as usual, meaning I looked no different than I did every other day of my life. I thought going as Posh was too much of a stretch, and I didn't have the confidence to even attempt it.

When I got to the party and saw Sierra dressed up in this tiny dress, with her long blonde hair shining in two high ponytails, I was in awe. She looked just like Baby Spice, and as I went inside, I saw that so many of the other girls looked just like their favorite Spice gal too. Sierra remarked that I should have gone as Posh. I could have worn a black dress and borrowed a pair of my mom's high heels. I shrugged at her, sheepishly went into the party, and tried getting the popular girls in my grade to talk to me. Rachel was so nervous about going to the party that she got a stomachache and ended up staying home. So there I was.

Sierra opened her gifts, and one girl gave her a kit full of makeup, so naturally she wanted us all to explore this crayon box full of goodies. I took a pencil, which I would learn many years later was eyeliner. I had no idea what this mysterious blue pencil was or how you used it, but I remembered my mom using one somewhere high up on her face. I took the navy-blue pencil and colored in my eyebrows. When I emerged from the bathroom, Sierra practically spit out her fruit punch.

"What happened to your eyebrows?" she said.

"I colored them in; isn't that what you are supposed to do with that thing?" I asked.

So now my bushy, Oscar the Grouch eyebrows (as my cousin Kelly had once referred to them) were a navy-blue hue. I scrubbed ferociously to get the ridiculous color out of them and went to the living room to have pizza.

The school year went on, and then summer came and I spent long days swimming in my pool and reading *Teen People* and *YM* magazines. Rachel went to a nearby camp for a few weeks but she was home every day by dinnertime. Sierra and Rachel also had pools, so we each took turns having swim dates and sleepovers; then we ran to the mailbox each day to check whether our middle school schedules had arrived.

The day mine did, I ripped open the envelope as fast as I could and dialed Rachel's number. We had *no* classes together. I called up Sierra, and it was the same diagnosis. My older cousin Anthony (Ant) had just graduated from our middle school and was now on his way to becoming a freshman at our high school, so he came over and marked up my schedule with little checks next to the names of "good" teachers and little *x*'s next to the names of "bad" teachers. But I still wouldn't have my two best buds with me when school started. So the three of us waited patiently for our lives to change in middle school.

Within two weeks of school starting, I got my period for the first time. I think this had to do with how stressed I was about having so many kids in one building and having to run from class to class within a short time span. Middle school was rough, and each night I had trouble falling asleep, because I was anxious about what the following day would bring. I can still close my eyes and picture walking up the steps in my old middle school and trying as hard as I could to open my locker. Middle school is rough for anyone except, of course, the popular kids. I used to wail, "But everyone else is getting their hair colored like Britney Spears and wearing sexy clothing like her!"—to which my parents told me that no means no. I look back now and understand where they were coming from. No twelve-year-old should be dressing up like a vixen.

The first class of my middle school career was English, and I can still see the teacher's smiling face and her blonde hair shining brightly. She made class fun, and while there were no kids in the entire class from my elementary school, I liked laughing at the jokes of the new, funny boys in my class.

I actually didn't see many of the kids I had grown up with throughout the day. My middle school had many students, and therefore it had two teams to break down each grade. I was on a different team from Rachel but on the same one as Sierra, but really I saw the two of them only in passing. I didn't make many new friends, like most of the other kids did.

I became really friendly with a girl, Sue, in all my classes, and we passed notes back and forth and studied together, but she wasn't allowed to go to the movies or the mall because of her strict upbringing and family's culture.

While girls in my grade were going on double dates to the movie theater in town, I spent my spare Saturday nights on my godmother, Aunt Jo's, sofa. She lived across town and had the best snacks, so each weekend was a fiesta. We would order a pizza and watch a movie and then on Saturdays, after we slept late, we ate endless bowls of sugary breakfast cereal in front of the television and then went to a flea market or to visit a friend of hers.

Her three daughters—Jo Jo, Kelly, and Angie—would give me a French braid and jazz it up with bows and headbands. They were the older sisters I'd never had, and I loved it. They made me feel so cool with how they painted my nails (which always got my dad mad when I came home) and teased my hair. In return, I gave them back massages.

Sixth grade was a whirlwind and over before I knew it. It was a year of so many changes, and then it was time for the hot summer. Freedom! Days to be spent lying by the pool, eating chips, and going to Girl Scout camp with Rachel.

Then enter September 1999: seventh grade. Remember how I said the start of sixth grade was rough? Seventh grade was even worse. This time I was fortunate enough to have a few classes with Rachel but once again, none with Sierra.

Regardless, middle school was rough. Oh, did I mention that was the year I got braces? I would have those pesky suckers on for three years. *Ugh.* Flared jeans were back in style, and so were Old Navy tech vests; Rachel and I got matching blue ones. My mom took me shopping and let me pick out my very first pieces of makeup. I picked out brown lipstick, rosy blush and a powder-blue eye shadow.

I also begged for a pair of platform white sneakers, which all the cool kids were now sporting. The shoes were so elevated that they were hard to walk in, and one day as I walked down the staircase leading to the front of the school, the lace came undone, and I tripped and went flying down the staircase. I landed face-first on the ground with my backpack smacking me in the upper part of my back, and just as my dignity was flying out the window, the hot sixth-grade social studies teacher appeared and screamed, asking whether I was all right and alive. I'm not sure how I didn't break every bone in my body or my face, but I survived. I got off the floor, brushed myself off, and tried to ignore the fifty or so students on the staircase as well, who were rushing off to their next class. The same tripping scenario happened at least three more times throughout seventh grade until I finally got the hint and donated those god-awful shoes to the Goodwill.

A few weeks into the school year, my dad dropped me off at Rachel's one Sunday afternoon so we could study together. I noticed a box hanging on her door and asked her about it, but she said she didn't know what it was. A few days later, she sent me an instant message on AOL and said she had big news to tell me in school the next day. I thought it was something to do with the handsome jock I still fancied a year later. Not exactly. At school the next day, Rachel, never one for too much excitement and commotion, blurted out, "My dad got a new job—we're moving to Pennsylvania."

Time seemed to stand still. The crowded hallway suddenly became a blur; all I saw were bodies whooshing past me and up the staircase in front of us. "I gotta get to class … Call me tonight for more details!" And off she went.

I couldn't think straight for the rest of the day, and the first thing I did when I got home was run past my mom's office and leap onto my bed to cry. She came in to see what was wrong, and I blurted out, "Rachel's dad got transferred, and they are moving!" My sobs grew louder as my pillow became damp.

"I worried this day would come someday. She is really your only friend. I wished you would have made friends with some of the girls in your class," my mom said.

Easier said than done. I'd asked a girl on the local basketball team I played on the summer prior whether she wanted to get together one day, since we hung out a lot at the practices. When I went to ask Jo Jo (who came to watch me in action) for a pen and paper to get the girl's phone number, the girl said, "I really can't give out my phone number, because my parents told me not to give it out to strangers." Ouch. That was about the extent of my existence trying to meet new friends. I talked to other girls in my classes, but they all lived on the other sides of town and had strict parents. So Rachel was my old friend and the best one a person could have asked for. Middle school is cruel enough, and now I wasn't even going to have a single friend. The world was becoming a lonely place for me.

Rachel was moving in a month; her dad worked for a large company, and they were transferring him to a branch two and a half hours from where we lived. Her dad had to report to his new job immediately, so he found himself an apartment while their new house was being built. He lived in his apartment from Monday to Friday and went home for the weekend from Friday nights to Sunday nights. Rachel's whole world changed in a matter of days. She was suddenly packing up her boxes and gearing up for her last days as a New Jersey resident. I, on the other hand, was going insane. How was I going to spend my weekends? Whom would I walk to the bus line with every day and call on the phone each night, discussing every detail of the latest NSYNC music video?

We celebrated our last Halloween together, dressing up in matching baby costumes, complete with pacifiers in our mouths and pigtails in our hair. Another girl in her neighborhood came over dressed as Britney Spears in her "Baby One More Time" video to go trick-or-treating with us, and off we went to pick up Sierra and get some candy. Our last Halloween as a large group was sad, but we tried to make the most of it. Sierra had just gotten a dog, so she showed him to us when we got there. Halloween was fun, but it only brought us closer to Rachel's departure.

My mom thought it would be a good idea to throw Rachel a surprise going-away party in my basement and invite all our friends. I love planning events, so I made a guest list of girls in our Girl Scout troop and ones living in her neighborhood. I also love to bake and was oozing with excitement just thinking about all the goodies I could whip up for this party. I rented movies and CDs, blew up balloons, and was ready for a party I wished I never had to throw in the first place. If only she could have just moved in with us and stayed in the middle school with me so I had someone to hang out with during the most awkward phase of my existence.

Rachel thought we were just having a girls' night in and watching *Selena*, so she came to the party dressed casually. I put on my brown lipstick, topped with lip-gloss for an extra shine. What can I say? I was still aiming for that pop star look. The plan was for her parents to drop her off and for me to say I forgot to feed our dog, Bingo, so I needed to do that before we went out to dinner. Right after I said my little speech, Lin said, "No, but I just fed Bingo before!" and my mom shushed her before she could say any more. Down the stairs we went, and twelve girls jumped out to yell, "surprise!" Rachel never saw it coming.

And then she was gone. She cleaned out her locker, handed in her books, and headed for the Wild West. Well, not literally. She was only two and a half hours away, but that's still a lot for someone used to seeing their best friend every day. Her new house was gorgeous, perched atop a hill in a brand-new neighborhood in suburbia. She was very worried about fitting in at her new school and had many sleepless nights over it. I was a wreck, trying to go back to school and meet new friends when it was already November and the school year was in full swing.

I missed Rachel more than ever but was trying to keep myself busy. My mom signed me up for the town softball team again (the year prior Rachel and I posed in our matching red jerseys with our trophies after our last home game), and I was looking forward to it, but there was a mix-up in the paperwork, and I was assigned to a team across town. My town was so large; we had eight elementary schools, two middle schools, and two high schools; the organization was broken down by where you lived. Naturally, the year my best friend moved away, I would get put on a softball team across town with total strangers.

The girls on my new team weren't friendly, and only a few of them gave me their AIM screen name to chat after practices. I liked softball; back when Rachel still lived in New Jersey, I'd sometimes pitched while she was the catcher. It was like we were always in sync with each other. Now that I was on this new team, I got placed in right field, where I spent most games looking at butterflies and daffodils, waiting for the one time a ball escaped the first baseman's glove and came my way. The two coaches weren't friendly, and neither were their butch daughters. One coach held up my softball bag one day and snickered. "What is this? A lunch box?" While my family is affluent, we don't show it off. So while my teammates had Nike gym bags and Adidas cleats, I was rocking a bag my dad got for free at one of his work conferences, and I wore cleats from Kmart.

Middle school continued, and Rachel came back to visit each time she had a break from her new school; she was allowed to be a guest and follow me around all day to my classes. She loved being back in our school, and the teachers and our fellow classmates liked seeing her. Our parents picked a halfway point, and that is where we met up before one of us climbed out of the car and got into the other. After so many trips to New Jersey for long weekends, it was my turn to go to Pennsylvania for my trip.

"Wait until you meet my new friends—you're going to love them!" Rachel squealed. I casually stated that I was more than happy with just hanging out at her house and having her mom drop us off at the movie theater for a night out; I didn't need or want to meet her friends. She got upset and asked why I kept avoiding the subject. Truth be told, I was jealous of them. People in her new state are a lot friendlier than people in my home state, and while I was having trouble meeting friends, she had just moved and had already made a nice circle of friends. The situation made me want to cry into my pillow all night.

I broke down and met her new pals, and they were friendly. They led very different lives than those of Jersey girls, so we had different interests and hobbies, but nonetheless, they were innocent and fun, just like Rachel. She joined Girl Scouts again and was doing all sorts of weekend activities with her new friends, and I was trying to be happy for her. We wrote each other long, hand-written letters each week and were allowed to talk on the phone every week (after nine o'clock at night or on weekends when the call was free).

I started breaking out of my shell and went to all the middle school dances with a few girls I hung around with. The first one I went to consisted of my wearing a black Backstreet Boy T-shirt I'd bought at my very first concert the summer before. While I didn't dance much, I had fun just singing along to Britney and Christina.

The following Monday in history class, a boy from my bus said he saw me at the dance. "You were wearing that Backstreet Boys t-shirt you always wear," he commented. I slowly learned that going to middle school dances meant a lot of serious preparation. By the time the next few dances rolled around, I was an old pro; my nails were painted a sparkly blue hue; my rosy blush was high on my cheekbones; and my powder-blue eye shadow soared about my eyelids. Still, no one asked me to dance, but it was all I hoped and prayed for.

Eighth grade was pretty uneventful, and before long, we graduated. The summer before high school was rough. I didn't have a lot of friends to hang out with; it was the second summer without Rachel being five minutes away, and I wasn't working or going to camp. I had a beautiful house with a pool but no one to enjoy it with. On most days, my Aunt Arlene and cousins Chrissy and Ant came over and swam with me or picked me up and took me to their house across town so I could swim in their pool. On other days, I invited girls from my grade over for a swim and barbecue with my family, only to never have them return the favor to me.

Then high school began. I was rolling with the big kids now. My dad taught me how to play tennis on the weekends, and I found I really enjoyed the sport. He used to get aggravated each time I hit the ball over the fence, saying the object of this game wasn't the same as the one in softball; the more lightly you hit it, the more in control you will be. My mom also came to the park, and we all played tennis as a family. Little by little, I got better and worked my way up to being on the high school team.

During preseason tennis, Ant stopped by one day to talk to my coach, who was his English teacher that year. Of course, he showed me around the place that would become my stomping grounds for the next four years. He was going to be a senior and would have picked me up every morning to spare me the cruelty of the bus, but he lived on the opposite side of town and would have passed the school to pick me up. Ant was also late for everything, so his picking me up and our getting there by 7:50 a.m. would have been pretty interesting.

So on that hot August day in 2001, a week before school started, Ant waited for my tennis practice to end, and then he did a walk-through of all my classes with me so I wouldn't get lost on the first day. He once again told me which teachers were good and which were "evil" (and with whom to avoid eye contact). But nothing fully prepared us for what would happen during the second week of my high school career.

School had been in full swing for only about four days, and the weather was so hot. I wore elastic-waist jean capris (I couldn't fit into most pants with buttons and zippers) and a red t-shirt with a heart in the middle, as if it were still a scorching July day. September 11, 2001, was a beautifully warm day, and with no air-conditioning in the high school classrooms, it made for a tough atmosphere to focus.

I was sitting in English class when the principal came on the loudspeaker, asking the teachers to "please turn on the televisions regarding the attack on the World Trade Center." Within minutes we saw a burning tower with black flames engulfing the sky around it. My teacher, a pretty blonde newlywed, put her hand to her mouth and ran out of the classroom. Another teacher came in to watch us for the rest of the period; we later found out that the newlywed's husband worked in one of the towers, and she needed to find out whether he was okay. It turned out he was.

The period ended, and I looked for Ant in the crowded hallways until I saw him. "Did you see what happened?" I asked, and he nodded, in shock himself.

Living in northern New Jersey, my family always went into "the city." We went every December to see "the tree"; we went there for dinner on some Saturday nights and to the Museum of Natural History with family friends. My parents were cultural and also drove into the city on many Friday and Saturday evenings to meet friends for dinner and drinks, while my Granny and Poppy babysat us. My dad used to work in the World Trade Center too, when he and my mom were newly married. I remember hearing stories about how they ate at the Windows on the World, the famous restaurant atop one tower. My dad took us to the World Trade Center one winter evening after we saw the tree at Rockefeller Center. He wanted to show us where he worked, and I remember him telling us to lean against the building; and on windy nights, such as that one, you could look up and see the tall buildings swaying slightly in the sky. It was fascinating to put your entire body against a skyscraper of that magnitude and take it all in.

After Ant went his way in the halls, I was forced to go to PE (my favorite), but to my luck, the bleachers were down, and TVs were rolled out. We were told we didn't have to get changed that day. Instead, some of the older boys played basketball, while the rest of us watched the TVs in horror. It was in that very gym class that I watched the second plane hit the other tower, and a short while later, I watched the towers crumble in a pile of thick, black smoke.

I remember that day like it was yesterday. I came home to an unusual sight, consisting of my parents sitting in the living room, their eyes peeled to the TV. I curled up in our other living room and called Ant, like I had done so many times before, to chat about how high school was going for me. This time the phone call was a little different.

"You know who was in the towers, don't you?" he asked, and I shook my head into the phone. "Kelly's best friend ... She worked for Cantor Fitzgerald." Kelly had brought her best friend over to my house many times to swim and tan by our pool over the years and to ride in my dad's sailboat during the summer months. Her best friend had been like family; she was a pretty girl who was newly engaged. Just the weekend before, my cousin had gone dress shopping with her for her wedding, scheduled for May 2002. She was only twenty-seven years old. She left our town to go to work that day and never came home.

The following weekend we went to a memorial service for her at our church; we walked across the entire parking lot afterward as the priest carried a framed photo of her. Someone tried calling her cell phone, and it rang, giving a false hope that left her family searching for answers. They never found her.

Days went on, but everything was a blur. I went to a football game that Friday night with three of my tennis friends (finally I had girls to hang out with), and as we drove down my street, people were on the corners with candles, singing sad songs and crying. Flags went up all over the country, and the newspapers continued to be about the terrorist attacks.

School went on, and I made new friends and was asked to babysit every other Saturday night for a family down my street. I made money and used it for trips to the movie theater with my new friends. The world was different now, and I was scared. Newark Liberty Airport, the one my family traveled out of when we went on vacation, was one of the airports used to carry out the terrorist attacks. Suddenly each winter trip my family took to Cancun now sent me into a tizzy, and I sweated the entire time we boarded the plane.

And just like that, I was officially a high school student. But life is funny. I grew up pouring through Ant's high school yearbooks each time I was over at his house, looking at the pretty senior girls with their fake nails and heavily made-up faces. They had the best clothes and hair, so naturally, I thought when I got to high school I too would blossom and look like one of these girls. It didn't exactly happen that way.

However, I was finally having progress in the friend department. While I saw Sierra throughout school and we carpooled to dances and school plays, we really didn't hang out much. She got a lot of attention from the boys in school (and even older ones, not in our school). Hello, hot, twenty-one-year-old pizza delivery boy? (It's a true story.) Meanwhile, I had a hard time getting boys to say my name correctly.

"You're Kristina, right? No, Kathryn?"

Sigh.

That summer, I was volunteering at my church's vacation Bible school for a week, when I met a girl, Sally, in the grade above me. I knew her from elementary and middle school, but our paths never really crossed until we were volunteers. She was an athlete like me and mentioned we should hang out when school started, and we were there early for preseason. We exchanged numbers (she had her own private line) and had a few sleepovers before school started. She was quiet and a little odd, but I couldn't be choosy with friends at this point. And did I mention that she lived in Sierra's neighborhood? So not only was she convenient to get to, but we also had similar interests.

School began and this new "pal" of mine was suddenly embarrassed to be seen with me in the hallways. Her locker was across the school, and a few times I went by it before school started to see why she hadn't called me back the night before. "What are you, my girlfriend or something?" she spit out. I just stared at her, speechless, and realized she clearly wanted to be "secret friends." On other days she talked and walked the halls with me, leaving me more confused than ever.

On the day of my first pep rally, she gave me red and silver star stickers to put on the sides of my eyes so we could bask in the glory of our school colors. All the girls in school did this on pep rally days; we were pretty good in sports, and our school had a lot of pride. Right after she gave me the stickers, we walked to the gymnasium, where a boy from her grade passed us with a few of his friends. I was so busy telling her a story that I didn't pay the boys much attention. She ignored my story and said, "Did you just hear what Justin said? He called you a pig."

Now, I have no idea why he would say such a thing; I never spoke to him or even looked his way. And just like that, that became the story of my high school life. Whoever felt like it called me fat, and I never said or did anything. I never told anyone because I didn't know I could or should. People constantly gave me a hard time, whether it was the kids in my grade calling me by the wrong name or my getting ridiculed for my size. But I was shy and kept on doing my thing, knowing one day I would leave those people behind in that town and better myself.

Freshman year came and went, and before I knew it, it was graduation day, and I was sitting in the stands with my aunt and uncle, cheering on Ant as he graduated. I would miss him after he was gone; I felt safe having him in the school with me, and I really liked seeing him throughout the halls and sharing the same teachers.

Sophomore year was pretty uneventful; it was the year of sweet sixteen parties, and suddenly, I was getting invited to them. I wanted a boyfriend so bad and had a huge crush on a senior guy. He was a baseball player (I played softball), and he had the cutest smile and wore clothes right out of a Gap catalog. His brown hair, smile, and tall, athletic build made me swoon. Oh, I was in love, all right. The one and only time we actually had an encounter was when he bumped into me at my locker while running by, late to history class.

"I'm so sorry!" he said as he glanced over his shoulder after almost knocking me over.

"That's okay … you can do it anytime!" I blurted out.

I had a great time playing tennis in the fall but couldn't say the same for softball in the spring. I'd always played softball while growing up, but as my mom used to say, "You hit the ball so good but have trouble running to the bases." Ant had the same problem when he played baseball while growing up. I would huff and puff while running the bases, so my coaches always plopped me in right field, where little action occurred. My afternoons consisted of watching the sweaty baseball team make their way to the locker room showers after practice.

I started to hate softball. I hated watching the popular girls parade around in the locker room in their thongs while they sipped SlimFast shakes, while I changed in the corner and prayed no one looked at me in my extra large underwear. I didn't fit in, I had only one friend to talk to, and the days when she wasn't there were hell because I was alone. None of the girls were mean; they just ignored me every single day.

I finally quit softball during my junior year, and it was the best thing I ever did. The last straw was when I spent an entire Saturday afternoon at a nearby park for our doubleheader, only not to play ... at all. My mom came by to bring me some food so I didn't have to buy the junk they sold there, and she was really mad when she found out a sophomore was going to be playing right field for the second game, and I was going to be benched. She told me to ask my coach whether I could go home, since I had already been at the park since ten o'clock, and it was now almost four o'clock.

"Leave? Why would you want to leave? You should be supporting your teammates!" he bellowed.

So I stayed. That Monday morning I marched into my female coach's office and told her life was becoming too much with my part-time job at a nearby bagel shop, schoolwork, religious education classes, and softball. Something had to give, and I'd chosen softball. I handed her my uniform, and she said, "I hope you're making the right decision." I smiled and walked away. It was one of the first big decisions in my life, and I'd made the right choice. It felt good to find my voice and put my foot down.

It was also during high school that my family began to take two vacations a year. While I dressed pretty cheap, my family used our money in other ways. We had a beautiful house with a kidney-shaped, in-ground pool (which a friend later told me meant I was rich). I loved traveling with my family; we ate fine cuisine and visited exciting places. My dad had been to forty-eight of the fifty states for his business trips, a goal I wish to achieve in my lifetime. Each time we went away, he mapped out the best eateries and directions on how to get to historical landmarks.

When we went to California one summer, we drove over the Golden Gate Bridge, walked Fisherman's Wharf, and hiked Muir Woods. Another year we headed to Seattle, went whale watching, and had the freshest salmon I ever tasted. We talked to people from all over the country who loved the fact that our dad brought us on his business trips and turned the rest of the week into a family vacation. We toured the Grand Canyon, hiked Devil's Tower in Wyoming, and asked the concierge what there is to do in Rapid City, South Dakota (turns out there's nothing to do in Rapid City, South Dakota). We were mature from all our travels and became seasoned tourists.

Therefore, we were no coach potatoes. My dad wasn't a fan of lazy people who sat around all day because at our house we always had so much to do. We spent many of our weekends working on the outside of our house, either raking leaves or fixing something. We also hung the clothes on the line to dry during the summer and autumn months. *Spoiled* was not a word in our vocabulary. It was this hard work that made our vacations so much more special. They were a chance for us to turn off our cell phones and laptops in exchange for playing beach volleyball and sipping margaritas poolside.

While we had so much going for us, my dad wanted more. Our house was the biggest among everyone we knew, and we always received compliments on our football-field-sized backyard. During my junior year, my parents sat us down and announced that they wanted to move to a different town. After living in our house for over twenty years, they wanted a change and thought a bigger house in a new area was the way to do it.

So we began looking at houses on the cold winter weekends until my parents settled on a brand-new neighborhood about twenty minutes north of us. There was room for one more house to be built, so just like that, builders started to create our dream house. My brother and sister started fresh at the new schools (Lin was in fifth grade, and Mikey was a freshman in high school) that September, but I was able to commute back and forth because I had a car. Just like that, life changed once again.

My dad (being an engineer) calculated everything down to a science. He designed our house exactly to his liking, and my sister and I were so excited to share a large bathroom with two sinks and have not one but two staircases.

As the building of our McMansion occurred, our family started to notice problems with Ant. My aunt and uncle threw him a large surprise twenty-first birthday bash at a local hall, but he disappeared after most of the guests left to hang out with some "new friends." As my family stayed to help clean up, I saw his new crew pull up to take him out somewhere, and they looked like trouble. A week after his birthday, he called me one evening to chat, but it was at the exact same time as my favorite TV show, *The O.C.* He called right in the middle of it, so I hit the "ignore" button on my flip cell phone and told myself I would try him another night during the week when I wasn't so tired from tennis and homework. I never got the chance.

A week later, the phone rang in the wee hours of the morning, jolting me out of a dream. I didn't have a house phone line in my bedroom, and I wondered who was calling at such an odd hour. And why was no one picking up the phone? The phone rang until the answering machine kicked on, and I heard someone yelling into the machine, begging us to pick up. I was exhausted from school and tennis, so I rolled back over, hoping someone else would answer or play back the message. The next morning I went into the kitchen, and as I groggily rubbed my eyes, the first thing I asked my mom was, "Who called last night?"

Her expression was hard to read, and she instructed me to wait until Mikey and Lin came into the kitchen. Suddenly, my dad emerged and told all three of us, "There was an accident last night, and Ant is dead." The words cut through me like a knife.

How could someone I just saw be dead? I was confused and felt sick. My dad wasn't an emotional man, so there were no high-pitched cries or tears rolling down his face as he presented this news to us. Therefore, I almost thought there was a mistake. Or perhaps I was sleepwalking as I sometimes tend to do. There was no way in hell this was real. The first best friend you ever had isn't supposed to die on a random weeknight during your senior year of high school.

My parents announced they were leaving to pick out flowers and help my aunt and uncle make funeral arrangements. They told me to stay home from school, since word would quickly spread about what had happened to my cousin. My mom dropped Mikey and Lin off at school, since they were attending schools in our new town, and no one knew Ant. Plus, they thought it would be good for them to focus on something before they were out of school the rest of the week for the wake and funeral. So I stayed home alone, with strict orders not to drive (they were worried about me being distraught and getting into an accident) and not to use my cell phone in case my school friends tried calling me. So what did I do? I scrubbed the bathroom toilet while playing a Clay Aiken CD. At the time, it seemed like a good idea. I wandered around aimlessly, eating cookies here and there and just being in a fog until I decided to turn on my cell phone. I turned it off each night before bed, so the phone had been off since nine o'clock the previous night.

I immediately got a slew of voicemails from concerned friends at school, and I felt a wave of sadness, knowing they were just as shocked as I was. While my parents had told me not to call anybody, they didn't say not to pick up if someone called. Sierra called shortly after I turned the phone on, and I hesitated and then decided to pick up.

"Katrina! Where are you? I'm here in the hallway at school, and a few of us just wanted to call and see how you were doing. I have been trying to call you all morning ... Is it true about Ant?" she yelled into the phone, practically breathless.

I told her it was, but I didn't even know myself what had occurred, so I was certainly not at liberty to say that to her or anyone else. I said I was fine but wouldn't be coming into school. I hung up and screamed at the top of my lungs. I screamed until it hurt. I cried and scrubbed some more, while turning up Clay a little louder.

My mom came home and hugged me really tight, saying she could never imagine what it must feel like to lose a child. And just like that, reality started to sink in.

Apparently Ant had gone out to a nearby park late that night, and the guys he was with (who didn't attend my high school—they were the burnouts in town) had persuaded him to buy alcohol since he was freshly of age to do so. They went to the local liquor store, Ant bought booze, and back to the park they went. It was a warm November evening, and from what we gathered, the guys encouraged Ant to chug vodka. Now, Ant never even drank red wine during Sunday night spaghetti dinners at Poppy and Granny's house, so he clearly wasn't one to down vodka in a dark park late at night. Ant was also on medication for a concussion he'd had recently, and since he never drank, he didn't know that alcohol and medication are a deadly combination. So, from what my dad said, the "vodka literally burned his insides"; and as he was choking, his pals got scared and ran off in different directions. Only one turned back to call the cops. Ant wound up dying en route to the nearby hospital.

Just as you never should prepare yourself to bury your child, you should also never prepare yourself to say good-bye to the first friend you ever had. Ever since I was a child, I always wanted to play with Ant and call him on the phone to chat about my day. Whenever the whole family went out to dinner, Mikey and I fought over who got to sit next to Ant at the table. He liked the same movies and toys, and we grew up idolizing him. The idea of him dying two weeks after his twenty-first birthday was unfathomable.

My senior year had just begun, and I had so many events to look forward to: applying to various colleges and eventually selecting one, picking out a pretty dress for prom, graduating from that hellhole, and starting myself off as a new person in a town far away. But suddenly, my world was shattered. Life would never be the same again, and I never, ever could have prepared myself for the pain I would feel after losing Ant.

Hundreds of people attended his wake; the line to get inside was wrapped around the block. There was an afternoon and an evening service, and many of the high school students and faculty took off from classes to attend it or came after school. I remember my relatives sobbing hysterically and Aunt Jo touching and hugging him, asking God how He could have done such a thing. At one point, she tried to climb into the coffin, remarking that it looked like Ant was sleeping. People my family hadn't seen in years appeared; the nurse at Ant's elementary school came. Coworkers from his job, students he'd helped mentor as part of his youth group, and basically all the teachers (good and bad) of our high school showed up.

Sierra stayed by my side and even went over to Poppy's house in between wake services so we could eat and break away from all the attention. Poppy's house was down the road from the funeral parlor, so we went there afterward, and people were generous and brought us deli platters, cookies, trays of baked ziti, and so much more. I remember biting into a brownie, and Angie looked at me and gave me a nervous glance.

"It won't go down; I suddenly can't swallow anything," I said. I started to panic, and she and Sierra both said my sudden case of swollen glands was a sign of stress and that it seemed I was having a panic attack. I managed to get the remainder of the brownie down, and back to the funeral parlor we went.

Ant's funeral was set for the next day at his church across town and directly across the street from the bagel shop where I worked. I remember one warm spring day; I had looked outside as I cleaned the glass windows and saw Ant. He had been planting palms in the ground for Palm Sunday just outside the church's sign by the street. I called him and jokingly said,

"Hey! I can see you!" He came over afterward, not wanting any food but just desiring to chitchat for a few minutes. And now, less than a year later, we were at the same church and saying good-bye to Ant.

I sat in a pew towards the front and cried the entire time. Later, my friend Veronica said she saw me crying, and the sight made her cry. The church was packed with teachers and students who'd opted to skip school. After Mass ended, we went over to the cemetery where my Granny was buried, and we laid Ant to rest a few rows over.

I went back to school the following day, and just as I had expected, the situation was incredibly awkward. People stared at me in the hallway, and teachers and classmates said they were sorry about Ant. I went from being someone who hated attention to becoming a spectacle. I found myself having little motivation to do much of anything, and seeing that tennis was finished, I went home from school and did basically nothing.

Sierra became my saving grace, coming over to take me to the movies or to get a pedicure when I really was quite content with just sitting at home, staring out my bedroom window in silence. One time she called me up to take me to a movie, and I said, "No thanks," since I was wearing sweatpants.

But she said, "So what? I'm picking you up anyway. Be ready in fifteen minutes," and off we went. I gained weight from lounging around so much, and I didn't have much else in life to look forward to; my family was mourning, and life was difficult.

In the midst of all this, my parents were busy watching our new house being built. I was sad to leave our old town, but this new house was going to be gorgeous, so I was excited. The entire street had glamorous houses with sprawling driveways and lush, well-manicured lawns.

But while the neighborhood was luxurious from the outside, the majority of the people in these homes were unfriendly. No one came over and welcomed us to the neighborhood except the people across the street (whom we invited over one spring night for appetizers only to have them never reciprocate the offer) and the girl next door, Jackie, who later went on to become a good friend of mine. What is so mind blowing is that my mom called the ladies on my block before we moved in; she asked where they had purchased their granite countertops and who had hung their chandeliers. They were friendly on the phone, yet when we moved in, nobody cared.

Two friends from my old neighborhood came to visit us one spring evening after we moved in, and although they both lived in very nice homes, they were in awe of our "Compound." I remember them giggling as I gave them a full tour, and they asked whether they could get married at our house—it truly was that beautiful. After my mom made us dinner, I suggested we walk around the neighborhood so they could get a glimpse of the other houses. As we made our way down the steep hill leading to the main road, a Jeep packed with teenagers whizzed up my street. We kept walking and were making our way back up the hill to get back to my house when they sped down the hill. Clearly, they didn't live in my neighborhood and were just out for a joyride. As they approached, one of them threw a soda out the window, yelling, "Rich bitches!" and then sped off.

My friends were horrified and immediately said, "What kind of people live in your new area?" I was shocked.

The warm months rolled in, and I was about to graduate from high school. I couldn't believe I was off to college … Such a momentous life event was about to occur, and I was so excited but terrified at the same time. Graduation day fell on Rachel's birthday and was an extremely hot day. I could see my family in the crowd (plus Chrissy, who was a sophomore in the school with me). I had sat with my aunt and uncle for Ant's graduation three years before, but now he wasn't in the stands for me.

While Veronica and others around me bawled their eyes out, sad to leave everything we'd ever known and to venture out into a foreign world we knew nothing about, I was ecstatic. High school hadn't been easy for me. It never is when you're fifty pounds overweight and have few friends. So I was quite ready to leave and discover myself elsewhere. After all the pictures were over and the good-byes were said, I drove off in my decorated car to Chili's, my favorite restaurant right in town. We had a great lunch, and then my dad looked at me and said, "Now what?" and I didn't know what to say. I had long days ahead at my part-time bagel shop job and shopping to do for my dorm room.

I had a few pool parties planned that summer and was picking out fun decor for my dorm room. I had every intention of going far away for college, and four schools accepted me. I liked the three schools that were far away and could see myself living there and being independent. But then Ant died, and I changed my mind, thinking it would be best to attend a local college.

My university was twenty minutes away from my home, one I had passed many times as a kid. My family drove past it when we went to dinner and each time we went to the city, because the train runs through the university. It was a small, private school that was in impeccable shape, and that impressed my dad during our tour. "Look at the fresh paint!" he commented as we walked through the athletic facility. The school definitely had wonderful perks: a strong alumni presence, easy access to the city, and well-manicured features that kept it looking beautiful. Compared to the old-fashioned Catholic colleges I looked at, my school had flair to it.

The night before I left for college, Jackie came over to hug me good-bye. Just as I was closing my front door, she stopped and turned around. "Katrina! Do you realize you could meet your husband in college?"

I laughed and said, "I guess I could!" And off she went, back to finish high school while I was off to the next best thing.

Everything in college was new and fresh, and I dressed up every day because first impressions are important. It wasn't until I would become a junior that wearing sweatpants to class became routine. I had an awesome roommate who was gorgeous and fashionable, but it all came with a price. She went on shopping sprees and came back with two sweaters and one pair of jeans, and her bill was $300. She took great care of herself, was on the Atkins diet, and always wore tons of makeup and put pink bows in her hair. Boys drooled when she walked into a room. Yet she was a nice girl, and we had a really good time as roommates.

I played tennis and was exhausted from matches and long bus rides home, but I had the best time laughing with my teammates and stopping at Wawa's for dinner. My dad came to many of my home matches and took pictures of me in action. I can still see his camera's lenses peering at me through the fence as I prepared to serve the ball.

I went home a lot on the weekends when nothing was going on at school, and my parents brought me back on Sunday evening after dinner. I worked at the bagel shop and babysat when I was home to make some extra money. I took great joy in being able to make myself food in my own kitchen and do laundry. Those are some of life's little luxuries you miss when you're living in the freshman dorms. Every Sunday night, my dad or mom helped me lug in my blue laundry bag and groceries; then we hugged, and they drove home without me. Lin missed me and sent incriminating cards with messages such as, "You better be coming home every weekend." So I made sure to go and call home often, and I always kept them in the loop.

In October of my freshman year, two high school friends, who also went to local universities, called me, because they had won tickets to attend a private screening of an Orlando Bloom movie in the city. They asked whether I wanted to attend, so I called my dad to get his thoughts. He was on top of a ladder, fixing something at my great-aunt's home, when his phone rang. He told me I could go, but since I had never been to the city without my family, I needed to be careful and call when I got there.

The girls came to my school, and we took the train, but once we were inside New York Penn Station, we were unsure which way to exit to reach the street. I saw a hot dog stand near one of the exits and had a flashback to the previous Christmas season, when we'd gone into the city as a family to see the tree. My dad had bought us all two hot dogs to share (yes, we were frugal like that), and as we passed the pretzel hot dogs among ourselves, Lin took a bite, and the hot dog plopped right out and landed on the floor. We watched it happen in slow motion and simply stared at the wiener lying on the dirty floor in the middle of Penn Station. My dad was pissed off; he'd just paid six dollars for that pretzel hot dog, and there it was. Lin got upset, and my brother and I rolled our eyes and remarked that these things always happened to Lin because she was so clumsy.

Seeing that hot dog stand helped me remember where to exit the station, so that is how I led us out that night. I felt so grown-up to be walking around Midtown Manhattan on a weeknight, and I wore the only pair of high heels I had brought with me to college. A group of construction workers whistled at us as we walked down the street.

I went to the city a few more times that year to see plays through the school, and slowly but surely I began to fall head over heels in love not only with New York City but also with college life in general. I felt grown up and had professors who really took the time to get to know their students, and I was joining clubs and making new friends left and right. No one knew me as a shy former fatty, and I really liked that. I was blossoming as a whole new person, and life was really becoming sweet. If I'd had my way, freshman year would have never ended.

But as I came to realize, nothing is ever as it seems. Just as life was finally turning around for me, my freshman year ended, and I moved home. After being home for a week, my dad got diagnosed with skin cancer. Back in February, he'd noticed an unusual lump on his neck and wondered whether it had somehow come from our trip to the Dominican Republic that January. He went from doctor to doctor, getting opinions; he and my mom rode the Amtrak train to other local cities to speak with different doctors. They found out that his internal skin cancer was quite rare, and he began to fight it.

My mom and Poppy drove him to the nearby hospital for chemotherapy and radiation. We watched him become easily fatigued and lose his appetite; he wondered aloud who had put a whammy on him and why this had happened to him. Italians are superstitious people, so he often wondered whether someone close to us was jealous of our fortunes and had put a curse on us. His friends came over to see him, and we continued on; my mom went above and beyond to buy him protein shakes and make him Jell-O and pudding to help him gain weight, but nothing helped. He said it felt as if he were on fire from the radiation, and his appetite went out the window.

My dad was a heavyset man, but within a year he lost more than one hundred pounds. His legs looked like little toothpicks, and his face changed shape due to all the treatments. People stared at him when we were out in public, and he became defensive. The bump on his neck was fire-engine red from the radiation beating on it. He hated how he looked and no longer enjoyed going out. The few times he and my sister went to Wal-Mart, he used a cane to walk inside the store and used a motorized shopping cart to get around. My mom cried and spent time at the library, looking up books about battling cancer. My parents traveled into the city to try holistic treatments, where my dad received orange juice intravenously from a doctor who didn't take health insurance. That treatment didn't help.

Time went on, and my dad's condition worsened. He went on his final business trip to Arizona but needed someone to help him. We all went to drop him and Poppy off at the airport, and as we said our good-byes, my mom hugged Poppy and cried, saying to make sure he took care of my dad.

Poppy later cried as he told Aunt Jo how he had to help my dad tie his shoes and get him into the shower during the trip. His fifty-three-year old son was becoming helpless, and as much as it killed my dad to become like this, it was killing Poppy too. His body was no longer his body.

My twentieth birthday rolled around, and I picked a Mexican restaurant in town for dinner, and the night quickly went downhill. The rough tortilla chips got caught in my dad's throat, so he spent most of the meal choking on them, which was scary. At one point I tried to look away as he was choking, and he got nasty very quickly, asking whether I "had some sort of problem." We didn't go out to eat much after that.

As the winter of 2008 approached, my dad started taking matters into his own hands. He sold his beloved sailboat, the one we'd spent countless weekends on, sailing up and down the Jersey Shore. My mom traded her car in for one my dad could climb into more easily. And lastly, he sold his company, the one he'd built up from the ground and turned into an international, moneymaking empire. Years later I would come across a folder with cover letters and job applications for large corporate companies my dad had applied to. Not one of them had hired him, and many never even called him back. Years later, when he had formed his own empire and had clients all over the country who respected him and his work, I often wondered whether he said, "Guess who is laughing now?"

The cancer spread, and before long he needed a double hip replacement surgery at Memorial Sloan in the city. We drove in with Mom and Poppy very early one Saturday, which was nerve wracking for all of us, since we mostly hopped on a bus or train to get in. We entered his room, and he was hooked up to various machines and had a catheter. My brother cried, and Lin and I tried not to, but the tears came out as we waited in the hallway, when the nurse asked us to wait outside while she changed him. My dad later said he'd felt all dignity fly out the window in moments like that, and no one should ever have to experience some stranger wiping his or her ass. He came home fairly quickly but needed help moving around, and his bedroom became our guest room on the first floor, which required no staircase.

That autumn my parents took a scenic drive to grab some apple cider doughnuts and take in the fall foliage. The next weekend, we went apple and pumpkin picking as a family but invited my aunt, uncle, and Chrissy.

I had grown close to Chrissy in the years since Ant died, and right after he died, I was there to take her to the movies or to get her eyebrows waxed with me. She was always on the quieter side, but now her life was even more silent as an only child.

We always went apple and pumpkin picking, but this year it was a challenge. My dad wanted to ride the hayride but was unable to get his legs up the ladder, as he'd done every year before. It was a sin to watch him, and as usual, people stared, and we glared back at them for being so rude. My mom insisted she would stay back, waiting for us all to come back from the fields. Uncle Ant (my dad's younger brother) insisted he would wait with him too. We have some pictures from that day, and it's hard to look at them. My dad was losing his hair, so he wore a hat in the picture, and he seemed to have shrunk in size due to his hip surgery. His legs virtually changed in length and shape, and he clutched his cane in the picture, with a bandage on his neck, concealing the bump that had started this whole problem.

Winter blew in, with the usual snowstorms and bitter cold nights. We grew up overnight, it seemed. Now Mikey was in charge of chopping wood and loading it into our fireplace. When the fall semester ended, I was the one packing up my room to move home and loading it into my mom's car instead of waiting for my dad to help me carry out the large items.

That October I was leafing through a copy of *New Jersey Business Magazine* in my dad's home office and decided to give a call and inquire about interning there. The friendly receptionist connected me with the editor in chief who told me to submit my cover letter, résumé, and three writing samples. He was very patient on the phone, spelling out his name and instructing me where to mail the package. I was called in for an interview, so my mom picked me up and took me to it. I remember the outfit I wore, down to how long I spent straightening my hair for the sleek ponytail I opted for.

I nailed the interview and got the internship. It was three days a week, and they were willing to work around my class schedule. Since the internship was only twenty minutes from my house (opposite way from campus), I decided to move home and become a commuter. I toyed back and forth with the idea of living on campus and going to the internship, but this plan made no sense, because I would have been passing my area anyway. I loved my roommate that year and was active in my clubs and activities, but going home was the right choice.

That spring semester, Rachel was studying abroad in Austria. Eager to explore her family's heritage, she was ready to leave her large university in western Pennsylvania and head to Europe by herself. Over winter break we had plans to meet midway at the Flemington outlets with our mothers, but that morning my dad was too sick, and my mom couldn't leave him. I remember knocking on the doors to their bedroom, which were locked at the moment, and hearing some yelling and then silence. No one responded, so I pounded again, and my mom came out and asked, in an exasperated tone, what I wanted.

"Today is the day we are heading to the outlets to see Rachel," I explained, and my mom said there was no way she could go; I had to go by myself. Then she closed the door again. I would later learn that my dad bolted up out of bed to head to the bathroom but never made it. An accident occurred on the white carpet leading to their master bathroom, and my dad was crying, saying over and over, "How on earth did this happen?" And my mom was on her hands and knees, cleaning the mess. He kept apologizing, saying it was the lowest point in his life.

I was scared to death to drive to the outlets alone, since I hardly drove on the highways and preferred local roads. These outlets were an hour away, and I never drove to areas I wasn't familiar with. I wanted to see Rachel, so I did what I had to do; I hopped in my silver Hyundai Sonata to meet her. She was now taking both of her parents after I called her to explain that it would just be me that day. I made it there in one piece, and as I hopped out of the car to hug them, Rachel's mom told me to zip my purse and then went ahead and did it for me.

"You have too many nice things in there to keep open for the world to see! Zip it up!" she laughed. Her parents had matching warm smiles and easygoing tones. Their voices hardly went above a normal tone, and the one time it did, I never forgot it. They asked about my new internship and about how my home life was, and I faked a small smile and explained briefly what was going on.

All these years later, and Rachel and I still spoke on the phone about twice a month. Our universities were seven hours apart, but when we chatted, it was like old times. Our outing was meant to be fun, but I felt sorry for myself as we shopped, since my mind was elsewhere. I wished my mom were there like she was supposed to be, and then I felt angry with the cancer for ruining my dad's life and flipping our family life upside down. I just wanted to be a normal girl who made plans to go shopping with her mom, best friend, and her mom; but here I was, an hour away from home, driving on roads I was scared to be on, while my mom was home scrubbing her bedroom rug. It was a sad sight for all parties involved.

That chilly Sunday afternoon was the beginning of the end. Days later, Rachel boarded a plane and flew to Austria, and I missed her terribly. For the first time in our lives, she wasn't a quick phone call away. We would e-mail and connect on Facebook, but that was about it.

Shortly after she left, my family boarded a flight ourselves, this time to Fort Lauderdale. We were catching a Carnival cruise ship and heading to St. Maarten, San Juan, and to a private island to escape the New Jersey winter and have some fun in the sun. It would turn out to be our last family vacation as a group of five. My mom encouraged Dad to cancel it, but he didn't. As sick as he was, he refused to.

We boarded the ship and went to check out our nice room with a view. We unpacked and then wheeled my dad around the boat (he was now mostly wheelchair bound) and were shocked by how cold it was; the weather was unusual for Florida in January.

We did some activities during the week, but everything took longer with my dad. Getting dressed for dinner was no longer a quick "shit, shower, and shave," as he used to say, Now, getting ready took more than an hour, with my mom helping to shower him, dress him, and fix the large Band-Aid on his neck. We made our way down to the buffet, with my mom sorting through the Jell-Os and puddings, holding each one up to my dad; he gave her a thumbs-up or thumbs-down. He needed soft food; otherwise he couldn't swallow it.

Right in the middle of this, a classmate from college saw me and ran over. She was a year older than I, but we'd often had a good laugh in our classes together. She was on the cruise with her mom, and later that day, I saw her by the pool, and she waved me over.

There was a comedy club that night, but it was for those eighteen and over, and I really wanted to check it out. Mikey wasn't eighteen yet, so he was out. I wasn't going to hear some comedian tell dirty jokes with my parents, so I had to either go solo or ask this girl to join me. I chose the latter. We didn't have cell phones on the cruise, so we agreed to meet at ten o'clock just outside one of the main staircases. Right as I left our adjoining suite, my dad looked at me and told me to be careful. My mom later said he'd refused to go to sleep and was awake until I came back. I suppose going off on a cruise ship with a girl they had never seen before (and one I didn't know *that* well) was enough to keep him up.

In St. Maarten we got off the ship to walk around the town and boarded a taxi to take us to a nice resort. We didn't have enough time to swim, but we took some beautiful pictures of the scenery. No real family pictures were taken, although I have one picture of Lin and me posing by the water, and in the corner of the picture, you can see a tiny portion of my dad in his wheelchair with his cane; he's just staring into the horizon. Thinking about his life a year ago or about the next days ahead? I'm not sure. That picture is hard to look at.

Soon it was time to head back to New Jersey. There was a storm back home, and we ended up sitting at the airport all day long until the skies were safe again. The flight home was uncomfortable for my dad, and we had to be the last ones off the plane, as opposed to racing to be the first. It took him a while to get from the airplane seat into the wheelchair, which was nothing compared to how difficult it had been to get him through security earlier. The metal in his hips set off the detector, and when they told us he could go through a wheelchair-accessible gate, the doors to the gate swung open and hit him in the knee, causing him to curse and wave his cane around in anger. We got off the plane and headed home.

Within days my dad's health took a turn for the worst. I came home one day to find my mom crying in the kitchen, and out of the guest bedroom emerged our priest. He was well liked in our parish, and he knew all our names and faces. I can only imagine the types of words that came out of his mouth during that private conversation, and then my mind flashed to my dad and what on earth he must have thought and said in response. How do you prepare to die? How do you prepare to look your loved ones in the face and say good-bye? How do you leave this earth when you are capable of doing so much more?

Later that week, my dad started bleeding. I came home from my internship, eager to share the news on the articles I wrote that day and on how pleased my new boss had been with my editing skills. But I saw that my mom's car was gone and found my brother upstairs in my parents' bedroom. My mom had run out to Wal-Mart to get Dad large Band-Aids to stop the bleeding on his neck, and my brother was by his bedside, listening to him yell. The abuse was getting hard to take, with my dad whacking us with his cane, clapping his hands when he wanted something, or just yelling because he was in pain and we weren't moving fast enough to help him. The situation was hard to come home to.

On this particular day, my brother helped my dad upstairs, but as he lay there, bleeding, everyone was tense. I remember calling Sierra from my closed bedroom, and she asked, "Why don't you call an ambulance? He needs to go the hospital." I told this to my mom that night, and she kept brushing the idea off until later that night when she said no, that wasn't happening.

"Why? His neck is bleeding!" She said she and my dad both knew that if he went to the hospital, chances were, he wouldn't come back. They were right.

The Band-Aid helped his neck, and he was able to sleep in his own bed. Two nights later we had our cousins and aunts over to spend some time with my dad, and my uncle arranged for an ambulance to take him to the hospital. Dad was deteriorating in front of our eyes, and we were no longer able to move him. The local ambulance squad came up our driveway, and they carefully carried him from his bed to the stretcher. A few of my great-aunts came too, and before you knew it, we had about twelve people in the kitchen, silently watching this horrific scene unfold. That was the only way to describe it.

My mom came into the kitchen to grab her purse, since she and Poppy were about to board the ambulance, and she was fuming. "I don't know why you all came—this isn't some big show!" she said, and most were silent. But then someone spoke up and said they wanted to be with us as "Uncle Mike" left the house. It was around nine o'clock that Sunday night, and as the ambulance pulled away from the house, which my dad called his "paradise," there wasn't a dry eye in the house. My siblings and I went to bed and I went to work and my internship the next day, as if nothing was wrong. I thought a routine would be good. Instead, my mind was a million places elsewhere.

On a cold and wet February day, I was walking across campus when I got a phone call from my mom to get to the hospital as soon as I could. I called Sierra and filled her in, my panicked voice getting more hysterical by the minute. She asked whether I needed anything, and I asked her whether she could e-mail Rachel and tell her what was going on. Rachel knew more or less, but things took a turn for the worse so quick; plus her being in Europe meant we chatted only every so often.

I had my former roommate take me to the hospital. She was always willing to lend a hand when needed, and this was one of those moments. This hospital was about twenty minutes from campus. We got to the hospital, and she came in to say hello to my dad and then went to sit in the waiting room. His dinner had just been served, and whoever had thought fish sticks were an appealing dinner for hospital patients was also idiotic enough to forget tartar sauce.

My dad could barely chew bread without choking, and now he was going to munch on crunchy fish sticks? I called the cafeteria to have someone send up tartar sauce and was told it would be there shortly. I fluffed his pillows and blankets, and he asked what was new at school and at the internship. We made small talk, but I grew increasingly annoyed as the minutes ticked by with still no tartar sauce. I grabbed the phone and punched in the numbers for the cafeteria, asking where the heck the sauce was. My normally hotheaded father waved me off as I was on the phone, and when I hung up, he told me to relax, that it was all okay. He wasn't hungry either, but that was beside the point. I was done with incompetence.

He said he was tired soon after that, and I hugged him good-bye and left with my former roommate. That was the last night I ever spoke to him.

The next day, I got a call from my mom to come to the hospital after class but not to be surprised when I saw the state my dad was in. I went to Jo Jo's condo, and she drove us to the hospital, where we met up with our other cousins. She cried in the car, her wipers going full blast in the cold rain, and asked how I was doing. I stared into space before announcing that I was sad, and she said, "It's okay, baby," and squeezed my leg. She told me she was thinking of going to counseling to talk to someone about my dad. She'd worked for his company for many years and knew him on a more personal level; she'd seen him interact with customers daily and then also saw the side of him we all saw, a man on his boat having a few beers on the weekend. The man lying in the hospital bed wasn't that man. That lifeless man was victim to a disease that had ruined our lives in only a matter of months.

My dad never spoke again. I had seen him less than twenty-four hours ago, but now he lay in the hospital bed, thin as a skeleton, with his eyes glazed and not moving. It was a scary sight and one that was hard to take in. My mom, Poppy, and I took turns wetting a sponge on a stick the nurses had provided as a way to keep moisture in his mouth.

Poppy cried out, "Michael! Come on! What is the matter with you? Wake up!" in his strong, Italian accent. "He had some good meals these last few days; I was feeding him a lot," he explained to us, and my mom calmly said that a few good meals were a very positive plus but not enough to turn this all around.

We all sat there, one at a time, saying good-bye to my dad. Poppy pestered the nurses for more water, and my cousins went behind the curtain one by one to have some private last words with him. We went home that night, and my mom pulled us aside in the kitchen and said she wanted to "talk to us." Those are words no one ever wants to hear. She cried in the kitchen as she told us our dad was never going to come home. The skin cancer had spread to his spine, and that was basically a death sentence. He wouldn't be around much longer, and we had probably seen the last of him speaking or with his eyes open.

I always thought he was going to pull out of this. Always. So many people are diagnosed with cancer and live to tell their story and show their battle wounds. He wasn't one of them, and maybe I was naive, or maybe my parents had sugarcoated how bad his condition was, or maybe his condition had just rapidly deteriorated. I will never know. All I know is that I, never in a million years, would have thought I would lose a parent to cancer. Growing up, I barely knew kids who had divorced parents. It was basically taboo to have divorced parents in my town; the few kids who had them were whispered about, like, "Oh, did you hear about John's dad moving out into his own house?"

It was February 2008, and my dad would have been fifty-five at the end of the month, but he never made it. He passed away the next morning with all of us by his side. My mom and Mikey slept at the hospital overnight but insisted that Lin and I go home to get some rest. We didn't want to go home alone, so I went to Aunt Jo's, and Lin went to Jo Jo's. It was bitterly cold outside, so Aunt Jo and I slept in her large, messy bed. The blaring phone woke us. It was Uncle Ant. He told us my mom had called him and said to "get our asses over to the hospital." We literally jumped out of the bed, threw on the clothes from the night before, and within minutes he was beeping the horn outside her apartment complex.

He took us to the hospital, and it was a solemn ride down the highway. I don't think anyone spoke the entire length of the thirty-minute ride to the hospital. Mikey met us in the main lobby. He walked straight up to me, cried, and hugged me. He simply shook his head and said, "It's bad," and we all marched up the elevator and saw for ourselves.

There my dad lay, same as the day before. Before long our priest appeared and walked in the room to say a prayer with us. The man who spoke at the podium of a packed church on Easter Sunday and saw us sneak in late all of the time now came to pray with us. "Your mom called me," he said and winked at us to make us feel a tiny bit better. There we all stood, hands together in prayer, asking for forgiveness from the Lord for our sins and requesting a safe journey for my dad as he crossed into his new life.

Just like my dad had stood in the hospital room with my aunt and uncle four years before while Ant laid on the table, not moving and white as a ghost, now we were all in the room as my dad was passing. We were there when he took his last breath, with Aunt Jo reading the time aloud to the nurse, who wrote it down. We were in shock, but in the moments afterward, we walked out of the hospital with each other and the priest, and almost felt a moment of calmness. The hurt and pain were drifting away, and now we were just plain sad but in a calmer manner, without anyone hysterically crying or pacing the floor of a hospital, just waiting for the doctors to report more bad news. It was over. The battle with a rare form of skin cancer was over within two years, and now reality was sinking in. I no longer had a father.

We went home, and friends and extended family members called my mom; I helped clean the house and e-mailed my professors. Sierra was up to date the whole time, and when I told her I needed her to come home, she did. Without batting an eyelash, she called her mom and told her to drive the forty-five minutes to her university and bring her home, because

I needed her. She came to my house that night with a pizza, and before long, my college roommate arrived and so did Jackie, while asking what she could help with. I was embarrassed, but we had little food in the house, so I literally gave her our grocery list, and off she went to the store to buy everything. She came back with her friend, and they carried in a case of water, milk, eggs, and all the items we normally kept in the house; plus her parents sent over gourmet food from a place in town, so we had hot food.

Then out of the blue, Rachel called. Sierra had told her what was going on back here, and she bought a phone card and called, but I missed her; in the message she stated I couldn't call her back due to the card, so she would try me again and gave me the exact time she would be calling. I made sure I was free, and we chatted for a long while. It was so good to hear her voice; she always said the right thing at the right time. There is a reason she is my oldest friend, and that is because she has always been there as a voice of reason. I like to tell Sierra I am her voice of reason when she does crazy things, so we each fit neatly in this little triangle of ours.

Sierra stayed at the house pretty late that night, telling me jokes about things my dad had said to her or funny things we had done in school as kids. I, in turn, told her stories I had heard my dad tell others when I was growing up; they were hilarious. For example, once he was speeding and passed a cop car; he knew the cop was going to turn around and come after him, lights flashing, sirens blazing. So what did he do? He sped up as fast as he could, pulled into a driveway in the nearest neighborhood, turned the car off, and ducked down behind the wheel. The cop sped right past him, never seeing him there in the driveway. He waited until the coast was clear and then neatly pulled out of that stranger's driveway and drove home. Sierra roared with laughter, and I did too, but then I felt guilty for sitting on my leather sofa and laughing when my dad had taken his last breath earlier that morning.

The pain and suffering part was over, and my mom told us all that she'd worn makeup for the first time in a long time to my dad's wake and funeral. She mentioned the many nights after we went to bed that she'd stayed in the kitchen, making Mikey and Lin's lunch boxes, and cried as she stared out the window, knowing what was coming. She spent hours running to different pharmacies to order medicine for Dad, comparing prices and brands. Many summer nights, when I was home from college and able to help out more, she sent me to our local Wal-Mart to pick up his latest prescription. It was odd not having to do that anymore. It had become a routine to hear my dad choke across the table during dinner. Life as we knew it had changed completely.

My dad's wake had many guests from near and far, and we received plenty of food and flowers at the house. It seemed as if the doorbell never stopped ringing. Poppy had a hard time getting dressed for my dad's wake; he and my dad were close, and I truly think a big part of Poppy died that day. My dad was the one who did all Poppy's bills for him; the man never knew how to write a check, let alone read English. My dad took him with us to the shore on the summer weekends and down to the boat in the off-season to get it ready. Now there would be no more of that.

I must say that no one was hysterical at my dad's wake. Yes, we all wore black and were mourning, but everyone chatted with each other, and old friends reconnected. It was the way life was when my dad was around. Some of us even laughed at stories my dad's friends told; we heard about how great a guy he had been and about how much people had admired him.

When Jo Jo headed home, she tripped in the dark parking lot. She knew my dad was watching her, laughing, and saying, "You dumb ass!" Sierra, on the other hand, was smoking in the dark parking lot, due to being stressed over the entire chain of events. Suddenly, Kelly's cardiologist husband appeared and Sierra literally froze, cigarette in hand. He said hello to her then proceeded inside. "I'm sure it didn't paint the best picture, but I smoke when I'm stressed," she explained to me, clearly embarrassed over a doctor catching her smoking when someone just died of cancer.

On the day of the funeral service at our church, our priest gave a beautiful speech about boats sailing off into the horizon, and he knew my dad was on one of those boats now. Then one of my dad's childhood best friends went to the podium to give a speech. He started off by saying how much he was going to miss my dad and then said, "He was my best friend." He choked out the words, and there wasn't a dry eye in the house. I looked across the crowded church I'd grown up in and saw Sierra sitting in the pew, silently crying. Just the week before, when I'd called her after leaving the hospital, she'd cried on the phone, saying, "Katrina, you're my best friend, okay? You're the sister I never had. I'm closer with you than most of my family members."

She knew my dad pretty darn well, having been to the house so much while growing up, and she was hurting almost as badly as we all were. Then in the back of the church, I saw a few of my college friends and smiled, thinking it was nice they'd left campus and come. I also looked over and saw my two bosses from my internship and thought it was awfully nice that they'd come, considering that I was a new intern and the magazine always had deadlines.

When I returned to work a few days later, my one boss came into my small office, shut the door, and pulled up a chair to talk to me. He asked why I'd never said anything sooner and wondered how long my dad had been sick. Then he said I could take as much time off as I needed. But February was dragging on, and it was awfully cold; there wasn't much else for me to do, and I needed structure. My college professors also pulled me aside and told me the same thing; they were surprised to see me back in class so soon. What else was I to do? My mom was just beginning to handle everything at home. As chaotic as things had been, now things were quiet.

My junior year of college continued, and I managed to pass all my classes, work on articles for the newspaper, and hit the gym every day, all while working nineteen hours a week at a magazine. My communication professors always told us never to stop working; we knew we needed two internships to graduate, so once you knew your first one was about to end, you started gearing up for the next one. Some of my classmates didn't seem to understand this concept and wound up not graduating on time. They were too busy drinking at the Delta Phi Epsilon house to apply to more internships, I suppose. I was on top of my game.

I started looking and applying for internships right after my dad passed away, and then I saw it: an online job posting for an internship on Martha's Vineyard; it was an unpaid gig at the newspaper. My family has been going to the island almost every single summer since I was a year old. I know my way around that place like the back of my hand. It's small and quaint, and it's my second home. I had to apply, and I did. Shortly after that, I received an e-mail, saying they were very impressed with my writing samples. Could I do a short phone interview? I passed that with flying colors and got the job of my dreams.

I went to see my communications adviser, and as we sat in her office like we had done so many other times, I asked her whether she thought this was a sign from my dad. "Katrina, I truly believe so. Do you know how many students from all over the country applied to this? Hundreds, I am certain. And for you to land one, just like that, on an island you grew up on is not a mere coincidence."

So there I was. I was about to turn twenty-one and move five hours away for the summer, and I was ecstatic. I needed to find secondary employment, since the newspaper job was unpaid, but I began to envision a summer I would never forget. Spring rolled into early June, and it was right before my twenty-first birthday. My mom threw me a lavish surprise party on a boat that circled Manhattan while we ate dinner. I was so surprised and had truly thought it was a barbecue/party that my friend was dragging me to, for one of her friends from college.

I was floored when I walked in, and everyone yelled, "surprise!" Aunt Jo was among the missing, however, because she "doesn't do boats." I really wished she'd come, but I guess that was too much for her to handle. I also wished I would have put on more makeup, shaved my legs, and picked out jewelry. I lost my one earring in my friend's driveway as we left her house, so naturally I took the other one out. I wore a dress I wasn't crazy about, but it was stretchy, which was always a plus. And I didn't bother applying too much makeup or shaving because I was convinced the party was for a friend of a friend, so I thought, *Why bother?* Now I know for the future to always keep myself classy and ladylike, as Angie says.

The boat pulled back into the harbor, and we went home. After all the gifts were opened, a bunch of my high school pals and I went to see a horror movie. Then a few nights later, I went out to dinner with everyone before it was time to leave. I left two days after my birthday, on June 7, 2008. My mom and Lin drove me up, and we parked our car in the Woods Hole ferry parking lot like always, but this time with more bags that usual.

I wheeled my bike on board, and the rest was all up to our arms to carry. My mom cried as we approached land, saying she couldn't believe her daughter had landed a once-in-a-lifetime internship on Martha's Vineyard, and the man who had first introduced us to this magical place wasn't here to witness it.

The Saturday we arrived was sunny and warm. We hopped in a taxicab after exiting the boat, and it brought us to the house in Oak Bluffs, where I would be living. I'd looked on Craigslist for families to live with, and after talking to three, I'd picked this one. The other two offered rooms much farther away than where I wanted to be, and I knew the buses didn't run as frequently in West Tisbury, so that was out.

This family had posted a picture of the bedroom, and they wanted $700 a month. They lived past downtown, in a more country part of the island. There were trees and bike paths outside their home, and they were down the block from the middle school, where my dad and I used to ride to play tennis. One year I remember us riding there on our bikes, tennis rackets strapped to our backs, only to have it rain the whole ride back to the cottage, an unexpected summer storm. Memories like that never truly get washed away. So I was surprised we had never been to this area where the family lived, but mainly it was because we'd turned around and gone back after playing tennis. If we'd gone just five minutes farther, we would have hit a four-way intersection; their house was on the left.

The cab dropped us off, and we made our way to the front door, only to find a girl, who was a few years older than I, sitting on the porch and smoking. The house was very small and messy; old, rusty cars and tools were all over the lawn. In the backyard, a burnt-orange golden retriever howled, tied to a fence with a wooden rope as a makeshift leash.

We went inside and met Clara, the mother of the home. She welcomed us, riding in on her motorized scooter, which barely fit in the cramped living room. There was another dog, a beagle named Copper, perched atop one of the sofas; he wouldn't stop whimpering. Clara's son, Danny, emerged from a dimly lit hallway and shook our hands. He was the sheriff and said he worked the night shift, so on most nights, when I would be getting home from the newspaper, he would just be going into work. He was dating Caitlin, the smoker outside. She had a low-cut white spaghetti strap tank top on, with her large breasts bouncing as she came inside to welcome us. Tall but not exactly thin, she was friendly, and, my God, did she have a strong Boston accent. The words *wicked* and *smart car* would never be the same for me after hearing her pronounce them.

Nonetheless, we were a bit uneasy. We made our way to my "bedroom," which was directly across from the bathroom and next to Clara's room; it was also across from Danny and Caitlin's room. Apparently Caitlin lived with her family down the block, but she'd met Danny and was cuckoo over him, so she stayed here most nights. My room was very small, and the bed was tinier and shorter than the one I had in the dorm. But I had a closet, and they gave me a TV and a mini fridge for my room. I could share their large fridge in the kitchen, but they thought I might want my own, which was perfect. I chained my bike outside under the deck, next to the howling golden, Jake.

My mom and Lin slept on their living room sofas that night, and the next morning I rode with them to the center of town to have breakfast and find the office of the internship. Then they were off, about to catch the next ferry. I watched the large ferry get smaller in the distance. I was in the huge park, surrounded by the gingerbread cottages in downtown Oak Bluffs, where I used to run free as a baby. I sat down on a park bench by the gazebo and called Sierra. No answer. Then I called my roommate from college. No answer. I guess everyone was super busy back in Jersey. I wandered around the park aimlessly for a while then sat on a bench and had a good cry. I was nervous to be alone. Even in the dorms, when my roommates had left for the weekend and I stayed, there were people next door and folks wandering around campus I knew. Here it was just me.

I walked into town, bought my bus ticket, and set out to find a second job. The newspaper would cover my bus pass fee (forty dollars for unlimited rides per month) and my notepads and pens for when I would be out reporting and interviewing people for stories. My boss at the newspaper got his interns their second jobs at places where their ads were featured in our paper. He mentioned a sandwich shop I had always passed but never eaten in; he said I should go inside and ask for Al. I did, and Al was wonderful. A young guy with a heavy accent, he told me he could use help in his other store and that I came highly recommended, so I was hired.

I took the bus over to Edgartown, and around the corner from the newspaper office was the sandwich shop. I had worked at the bagel shop for so many years growing up that I was a natural at working with food and was excited to start. While Al managed the Oak Bluffs store, my boss in Edgartown was a tiny elf-like woman with dirty blonde hair and what else? Another heavy Boston accent. She once referred to our water fountain in the place as a "bubbler," and I never forgot it. She was interesting, to say the least, but made the place fun to work at.

I quickly got into a routine of being a workaholic, and although I was staying on one of the most beautiful islands on the planet for the summer,

I would be working way too much. But I had signed up for this and had done it to myself. I wound up staying on the island for two months and two weeks; I worked five days a week between the newspaper and deli. I spent my two free days at the beach or just biking around and taking pictures as I went. However, I also had to make time to do laundry, to go grocery shopping, and to write my articles and submit them on my laptop on my tiny bed in my cramped bedroom.

People were generous that summer, and I often walked out of the deli with fifty dollars in cash from tips I split with the other counter girl. Once or twice we each walked out with over one hundred dollars in our pockets. The newspaper was disorganized, and my boss had unprofessional tendencies, but I really enjoyed my time spent at Clara's house. Her family may not have had much, but they were loving people.

I messed up the bus times on the first Sunday night I was there. After our weekly newspaper meeting ended at eleven o'clock, I took my first bus back to Oak Bluffs, only to discover that my connecting bus wasn't coming. "It stops running at nine p.m. until the end of June, when the Island really picks up. Sorry!" my current driver told me.

I didn't know what to do and didn't have much cash on me to pay for a taxi. I was alone in the large park once again, and as I paced around, I thought I should call the house. I explained to Caitlin what had happened, and she said, "Don't even move! Danny will come down and get you in a few minutes. Anytime this happens, always call us!" Within fifteen minutes, he showed up in his truck for me.

I went home twice that summer, which was a lot for only being there a short while, but we had big occasions back home I didn't want to miss. One was Lin's eighth-grade graduation and Mikey's high school graduation, and the other was their large, double graduation party.

I had to figure out how to get home via public transportation, and it wasn't so easy, but I did it. I would leave on a Wednesday and take a ten o'clock ferry over to Woods Hole and wait there for thirty minutes until a Peter Pan bus came. That bus (way safer and cleaner that Greyhound) was my saving grace to get back home. I took that bus for a few minutes into the town of Woods Hole (by Cape Cod); it stopped in a parking lot, where I switched to another bus. Then I was on that bus the entire way to New York City, where I then got off in the Port Authority Bus Terminal and hopped on a local bus. This whole exchange took all day, as you can imagine, with me arriving in the parking lot of my bagel shop at dinnertime, where Jo Jo picked me up. It was so nice to be in my own house with my large bed and spacious bathroom.

I mostly spent time with my family and Lucky while home, and I made sure to lie by the pool and grocery shop for nonperishables, since the island was so costly. Everything was imported over on large tractor trailers, and there are only two small grocery stores on the island, so naturally the prices were jacked up. Once I remember paying four dollars for a bottle of ketchup. I nipped that in the bud real quick, went home, and bought a ton of food for my little kitchen area in my bedroom. I didn't travel lightly either; my mom insisted that I bring home my laptop and Coach purses each time I came home. I was living with strangers, but I trusted Clara and her family because they'd taken care of me. They always left lights on for me, and although they never asked when I would be home, I always volunteered that information so they knew where I was.

When it was time to head back, my backpack was filled, and off I went for my day of traveling. When I finally arrived back in Vineyard Haven that Sunday at about six o'clock in the evening, Caitlin was waiting for me. So many people were at the boat dock, waiting for loved ones to arrive, and it was so cool to have someone waiting there for me. She smiled and waved her arms so I could spot her. It was nice to be back on the island, and I was ready to report to the deli the next morning.

Clara spent most of her days knitting beautiful blankets on the sofa; she would enter them in the state fair in August, but I would be gone already. A widow, she was in her early sixties; her husband had passed away a few years before. He was the rock of the family and had built that entire house himself. They were married very young and had five children, but only Danny and his one sister lived on the island; the rest were all over. One day when Clara's eight-year-old granddaughter, Kaylee, was over, she asked where my dad was.

"He is in heaven, with Pop-Pop," Clara told her. Kaylee came over every day and slept over most nights. She was chatty, and although I found her to be a nuisance on the nights I was up late, writing an article, I would miss her when I went home. We watched movies together and did arts and crafts.

Call it what you will, but I made no friends that summer, so I spent the little spare time I had jogging or biking near Clara's house. I was in the best shape of my life that summer.

After I cooked my own dinner and they cooked theirs, we all sat on the couch and ate dinner while watching a show. Life was simple on the island, and while of course there are glamorous summer homes that cost $20 million, there are also smaller houses with everyday people living in them.

I went to dinner once with a coworker of mine from the newspaper, and she told me her life story; she was from California but was attending Brown University, so she decided to stay in New England for the summer. Somehow during the course of our dinner, she mentioned that she'd had cancer a few years back and lost all her hair. It was an awkward approach to end an already awkward evening, and that was the last time I would eat out with someone until my family came for our annual family vacation in July.

When they came, I slept over the condo we rented every night. I shared the large king-sized bed with my mom, the one my dad normally slept in, and ate my meals with them. It was nice to have time with them, and I met them at the beach a few times too; and of course they "surprised" me at the newspaper during our Sunday night meeting.

Summer went on, and then it was time to head home. I made sure to take off the last week so I could jog by the beach once more and grab one last ice cream cone before packing up. I went to the bank next door to the deli where I had opened up an account when I first arrived; I took out all of the money I saved up that summer. I hugged Sam, the friendly cashier I used to chat with during the mad lunch rush, and said good-bye to all the high school kids who gave me free ice cream.

It was time to go. Mom and Lin once again came, got me, and took a picture of me standing on Clara's porch one last time. Clara said I had lost "so much weight" from the time I arrived, and I looked great: healthy, tanned, and toned. I would miss eating healthy and burning off that occasional peanut butter cookie from the local bakery with a jog by the ocean. But it was time to head back to New Jersey.

I headed back just in time for my senior year. I had class only a few days that semester, so I decided to live back home to save money and work at the YMCA (Y). I missed living on campus; life wasn't the same as a commuter student. I missed being in the cafeteria with my friends, and it was a hassle to find a room to sleep in after a late-night meeting at the school newspaper. It was even more frustrating when I went from tennis practice to shower in the locker room, only to discover it hardly had any hot water. I usually packed meals for dinner to save money and calories, but eating alone in the commuter lounge or in my car was lonely.

I gained some weight that year and was no longer as thin and trim as before. I often ran from place to place, picking up extra shifts at the Y and then squeezing in a workout and shower before racing to campus for a meeting or class. As my senior year ended, we were in the "Great Recession," and the worst was only about to come. President Obama was our first black president, and I was graduating from college... with honors!

The year 2009 was in full swing, and before long I would take the stage with a thousand other students to get my diploma, only to have the president of our university call me "Christina." Sigh. Some things will never change.

As I looked in the crowded stadium for my family, my eyes darted back and forth until I spotted them. However, one person was missing. While my immediate family was there and so was Kelly, Aunt Arlene, Uncle Ant and Chrissy, plus Sierra and Veronica, Poppy was missing. He was supposed to be there, and I kept wondering where he was. My mom cried in the stadium and then cried some more during the pictures outside, saying how my dad would have loved to see his hard-earned money go to good use. We went out to eat, and then Sierra took me back to her house, and we got ice cream. I went home, and the phone rang; Uncle Ant wanted to speak with my mom.

She quietly came into my room a short while later, closed the door, and said she had something she wanted to tell me. The reason Poppy couldn't make it to graduation was because he hadn't been feeling well the last few days. He'd gone to the doctor, and they'd told him he had leukemia. I was shocked and felt like I had been punched in the gut. Illness had ruined another happy occasion in an instant.

Only a year and a half had transpired since my dad passed away, and now Poppy was sick. Poppy was in his early eighties but as healthy as a horse. He used to trim our hedges and pull weeds all the time for us; I would wake up and find him in our backyard, doing yard work at any given moment; and every time it snowed, he always called us to see whether we were okay.

That was May 22, and within a month, he was in the hospital, with an IV hooked up to him. I remember us going to see him on my mom's birthday (Fourth of July), and we could see the fireworks going off right outside his room. That was the first time we saw him in a hospital bed like that, and we all cried outside his room, not wanting to show him how scared we were. Aunt Jo and Angie didn't cry, and I truly believe they didn't think he was that sick, but we knew better. We'd watched my dad deteriorate very quickly, but this was Poppy. He never got sick and ate only fruits and vegetables. But seeing him like that was sickening.

We lost Poppy in the wee hours of the morning a few weeks later, on a hot night in July. I had just come out of kickboxing at the Y and saw a missed call from my mom on my phone. She said things weren't looking good and that I should head straight to the hospital. Sweaty and hungry, I ended up staying there with my family all night. Poppy was hooked up to machines and sweating in his hospital gown. He looked small and fragile, and his skin was an eerie gray color. We watched him take his last breaths until my mom had seen enough, and it was time to go home. It was just like the scene we'd witnessed seventeen months earlier in a different hospital, and we knew how it would end; we couldn't bear to witness it again.

We went home, and I took a midnight shower and went to bed. I woke up when my mom came into my closet to get something, and when I rolled over and asked whether Poppy had made it through the night, she said no. He was gone. I cried so hard at his funeral, and Jo Jo was the last one in the funeral home by his casket, begging him not to leave her. He was the father she, Kelly, and Angie had never had, and I think it was very difficult for them to say good-bye.

Losing three of the Musto men in less than five years has been mind numbing, and I would like to tell you I'm a stronger person for going through it, but I would give back all that courage in an instant to have them back. I would love to tell Ant about college life and for my dad to see me make the dean's list four times and walk the stage of graduation, wearing honor tassels, and for Poppy to see me pick up a paintbrush in my condo and actually paint the entire guest bedroom and storage closet.

Losing loved ones at a young age makes you independent, and as someone who always looked to others as an overweight, insecure adolescent, my adult self is pretty damn secure these days. There were so many things

I had to learn how to do by myself once the three people who always gave me their input were no longer here. My dad had taken me to tour colleges the summer before my senior year of high school and given his opinion. Lin and Mikey weren't offered the same courtesy. I took Lin to tour a college in Pennsylvania the summer before her junior year; going to Muhlenberg was my dream, and when I didn't get accepted, I was crushed.

I had flashbacks to when my dad had taken me there for the tour. As we'd entered the church on campus, my dad commented on the red doors and asked what the religious affiliation was. "Lutheran," the tour guide said. "What religion are you?"

And my dad said, "Buddhist." I got red in the face and whispered for him to shut up. Looking back, that was quite hilarious, but at the time, I didn't want any attention on us.

Ant had showed me around the middle school and high school and was always the first person I called when my class schedule came, since he loved to give me details on the new teachers I would soon face. And Poppy? Although he had hurt my feelings over the years when he commented on my weight, he was always there to pick me up at the airport or help me move into my dorm in the summers. He was the first person to show us how to properly pull a weed, and he often took over when I said I was tired or hot or just not in the mood to pull weeds. I once made him a steak sandwich out of leftovers in our fridge and brought it outside to him with chips and a water bottle, while he slaved away in our backyard. He told Aunt Jo that night on the phone that it was the best sandwich he'd ever had, and he kept raving about it.

"Sweetie, I don't know what you put in there, but it was all he kept talking about," she laughed. A simple man, Poppy ate well and had the body of a man in his forties when he died. He was in better shape than some guys I know. He was strict, and all his grandchildren knew better than to cross him, for his belt wasn't just an article of clothing he wore to hoist his pants.

Some days when I pull weeds outside, I look to the sky and curse Mother Nature for creating so many weeds. I truly hate pulling them, but when I'm done, I look around in pure satisfaction, knowing I accomplished something. I have a feeling Poppy is up there, watching me and saying,

"See! You're not a dumb ass! You could do it. Now if only your other cousins would do the same thing."

My mom says the one thing she misses most about my dad is his intelligence. He was not only book smart but also real-life smart. He worked in an office all day, but on weekends he was always fixing something with Poppy. If something was broken, they fixed it. I never knew what a handyman (or cleaning lady) was until I was older. We *never* hired anyone to do anything for us, unless it was paving our driveway or adding an addition onto our house. My dad fixed everything. We went to Home Depot so often that we knew the store pretty well. If the toilet, roof, or heating wasn't working, my dad took care of it. It's now that I feel how fortunate we were to have such handy men in our family, because when things break, we have to call around or ask for referrals; and you never know who you might end up with. My dad and Poppy hated the television and called it "the idiot box" for a reason. Too much consumption of it makes you fat and lazy. I would much rather read a book and can afford to watch television maybe only twice a week. Certain opinions stick with you.

I hate that when I was unemployed and trying my hardest to find a job in my field, I didn't have my dad or his connections to help me. He knew so many people who worked for fine companies all over the country, but he wasn't there to introduce them to me. I hate that he missed momentous days of my life, because a disease robbed him of every dignity he had left. My dad worked all day, every day; yet he still found time to take us to Home Depot or the local post office with him. He may not have been eating popcorn with me on the sofa, but that wasn't his thing.

They say bad things happen in threes, and they certainly did, starting off with my Granny and her two brothers passing away in the early 2000s, and then life was calm for a few years until Ant perished in the middle of the night. To be perfectly honestly, I hate having people feel sorry for me and treating me differently because I don't have a dad or because my cousin died in a peculiar accident at a young age. Grandfathers are expected to pass away eventually, but a little more than a year after my dad? That was a punch in the gut. Some say Poppy died of a broken heart over losing my dad, and I believe it. He and my dad were as thick as thieves, and I truly believe too much sadness can bring on disease, just like obesity is now shown to cause other illnesses.

Throughout all the deaths, I had my family nearby, and Sierra was there when I needed her. Rachel, although far away, was also just a phone call away. It is in your darkest hours that you realize who is there for you. I now understand why my Communications advisor, who encouraged me to head to Martha's Vineyard the summer before, told me she couldn't fathom how I got up each morning. There was so much sadness, yet I continued to function. Even years later, I will be in the car and hear a song that Ant and I used to listen to, and feel a sudden wave of sadness.

When there were times over the years when I didn't feel like living, I kept going. I got out of bed, put two feet on the floor, and thanked the Lord I was healthy and alive, and I kept going. I'm not saying that was easy, but over time, I was able to smile and laugh again. I was able to meet new friends and eventually find happiness. They say everything happens for a reason, but I will never know why these events happened to our family in such a short span of time. Time may heal everything, but I am still waiting.

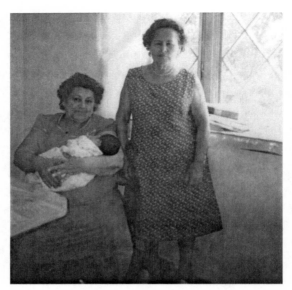

Granny and Baba doting over me as a newborn

Trick or Treating on Halloween with Aunt Jo and baby
Mikey. I loved The Wizard of Oz (although the flying
monkeys terrified me!) and was excited to be Dorothy

New Easter outfits for the Musto's! Mikey and I loved
the holidays because we had a blast playing with
Chrissy and Ant at Poppy and Granny's house

Girl Scouts was always an adventure and Rachel and
Sierra and I loved being together at the meetings

Each summer we went to Dorney Park and Kelly came to help babysit us

Dinner at the British restaurant at Epcot in Disney World-August 2005

All grown up at the Backstreet Boys concert the
summer we graduated high school

Poppy always came down the shore with us
and spent weekends on Dad's boat

Family vacation to London in June 2010. I love Europe
and London holds a special place in my heart.

All dressed up with Angie and Jo Jo for a family party; we clean up well!

Posing pretty in the November sunshine on Lake Norman

Lin and I mugging for the camera before heading to a fun wedding

Love

I fell in love in September 1998 during my sixth-grade English class. I had a crush on a boy when I was in the third grade, and it lasted until about fifth grade. But by liking him, it meant being too shy to ask him to sign my fifth-grade yearbook, so Sierra had to ask him. That's how I was for the first half of my life. I was shy, and the boy I liked in elementary school was cute and funny, so naturally I was fixated on him. But it was more of a schoolgirl crush, where I would knock on his door and sell his family Girl Scout cookies.

When he did sign my yearbook one year, he wrote, "You are so cool, man!" So I was a clown to him but not the girl he wanted to hold hands with on the playground. Rachel was the same way. She liked a boy from elementary school all the way to her freshman year of high school, and he had no idea. Sierra, on the other hand, stole kisses on the playground in fifth grade.

So there I was, on a hot September day, sitting in my sixth-grade English class, and there he was. He had dirty-blond hair, and he was on the soccer team. He had a knack for being a wiseass. He also had a knack for getting girls to fall for him; I distinctly remember seeing his name scribbled on a bathroom wall with a heart around it one afternoon while I was in the stall. It was huge, with arrows going through it.

Every joke he told was so humorous, every outfit he wore so sporty; and every time he said my name, it was like a song. Our birthdays were three days apart. We both loved the Yankees, played on the town softball and baseball teams, and were very good in our English and creative writing classes. We also had practically every class together in sixth grade, except gym (thank you, Jesus!) and home economics, so it was easy to fawn over his every move. I used to scribble his name in my notebooks and picture us falling madly in love. When you're in sixth grade, you think just because you like someone, that person will like you back, and you will go to prom together one day and live happily ever after.

One of the fondest memories I have of him is when Rachel and I were baking cookies (peanut butter, I believe) in our home economics class. He was in art class directly across the hallway from us, and his classmates were notorious for peeking their heads into our classroom as we were baking. On that day Rachel went to her locker outside our classroom, and lo and behold, he popped his head out of the art room to see what we were baking. She answered him matter-of-factly, and then he went on to ask whether I was there baking too. She said yes, and then he proceeded with "I know she likes me" as he grinned from ear to ear.

Instead of asking, "Well, do you like her too?" Rachel blushed, slammed her locker shut, and said if he wanted cookies from me, he would have to ask me himself. And off she went back into the classroom. That two-second conversation was one we recounted (and I replayed in my head) over and over for the next year. Rachel constantly said how much she wanted to kick herself for not asking whether he liked me too. She simply froze and didn't know what to say to him. I, of course, gave him the peanut butter cookies.

I continued to let him devour our baked goods for the rest of that semester. I baked, and he ate. Did he ever ask me out? No. The rest of middle school went, and even after Rachel moved away, he was still the main subject during our weekly telephone calls and the subject header in our letters back and forth to one another. He never did ask me out. Or call me. Or e-mail me. Or instant message me. Well, you catch my drift.

My first "date" occurred when I was fifteen, and boy was it a winner. Veronica was dating a boy a few towns over and wanted me to go on a double date with them. During one giggly IM session on the computer, we were chatting with him when it came up that he wanted to meet me. Sure, why not? So my mom dropped me off at Veronica's and asked why I was so dressed up.

"You look so pretty! Aren't you two just going out for pizza?" I was embarrassed to say we were going on a double date, so I left that part out.

I was wearing this short, navy-colored skirt, a pink top, and long, dangly pink earrings. And my hair was long and curly. Looking back, I looked hot that night.

So we walked to the Italian restaurant near her house, as I waited anxiously for the boys' parents drop them off. And, oh boy, did they. In walked my date with braces on, and the moment he spoke, his voice squeaked. Yep, somebody was two years younger than I and going through puberty. He was such a nice guy—a little chubby but overall very nice. I didn't know whether to laugh or cry when he asked me what my favorite movies and books were; all I kept thinking was that he still had braces on and that his voice sounded like Mickey Mouse. So I did what every other mature teenager would do. I said I needed to use the ladies' room, and "Uh, Veronica, didn't you mention earlier that you had to as well?"

So we both huddled in the tiny, one-person lavatory, called our other friend, and spilled the beans to her about my ridiculous date. She laughed so hard that she started to cry. The best part of the night? When we got back to the table, my date offered to pay for my tortellini entrée, but I insisted, "No, no, no. That's very sweet, but I have my own money." And I paid for myself. Even after all these years, I still kick myself for that. I should have just let the kid pay, but I just wanted to get the hell out of that place. The real kick in the pants would come ten years later when Veronica found my date on Facebook, and he had grown up to be attractive. You win some, you lose some.

The next guy I went on to like was two years older than I, and I too was with Veronica when I met him. My dad took Lin and I ice-skating on Friday nights during my high school years, and we were each allowed to bring a friend. After rounding the rink (holding onto Veronica with one hand and clutching the wall with my other), we noticed a high school hockey team stroll in for a late-night practice. I nudged Veronica, and we both couldn't help but stare. As the ice rink closed down for the night and I took off my ice skates, Veronica was fixated on the hockey team.

"Look at that one over there ... He definitely goes to our high school!" Judging by their red uniforms, they very well could have been from our high school and were there to practice. The one she pointed out did look a lot like a guy from our high school, a very good-looking, popular soccer player who moonlighted in the winter months by playing ice hockey. We zeroed in on his tall features and dark hair. Well, what we should have noted was that he was wearing a mask and was quite far away. Anyone could look like the captain of your high school soccer team from that far away with a mask on. It turns out this guy wasn't who we thought he was, but hey, he was cute, so what the heck? Veronica made a mental note of his jersey number and what high school he was from. She, of course, had a friend who had a friend who went to that same high school, so she did some "research" on him.

It turns out that he seemed pretty normal. He was older, which was such a bonus, and drove. We got his screen name from this friend of a friend Veronica knew, and before long we were messaging him and giggling as we did so. Eventually Veronica started dating someone else at school, and I had this guy all to myself. He asked me to go to a movie, and I remember meeting him at the theater to see a scary movie.

"It's because he wants to put his arm around you when you get scared!" all my friends said.

The theater was packed, and as we made our way to our seats, I thanked him for buying my ticket and offered to pay him back. I remember him saying, "No, it's really okay," and I asked whether he was sure. Ugh. I had no idea how to play it cool and was so tickled at the concept that somebody wanted to take me out to the movies on a Saturday night and potentially put his arm around me.

Well, the arm on my shoulder never happened. Neither did the fake-yawn-and-arm-around-the-shoulder move you see all the time in comedies. A surprise make-out session never occurred either. We basically just watched the movie and took in all the scary scenes. I had a nice time, but as we walked into the parking lot to head to our separate cars, we barely talked. I brushed off the silence by thinking he must have just been shy. We had our second date (if you want to even call it that) a few weeks later, but this time it included a mutual friend of Veronica's and mine. I was hanging out with this friend in the afternoon when he asked whether I was free for another movie.

"Can my friend come?" I asked, and in a way I was relieved when he said yes. I wasn't in love with this guy but definitely felt a tiny spark when I saw him. We met him in the crowded lobby of the movie theater, where he announced that he'd already bought the ticket. I was confused and started walking toward our theater when he said, "Well, aren't you going to buy your tickets too?"

I felt like such an idiot. My friend and I went and bought our tickets. I forget what movie we saw but remember it as being a somewhat fun evening. I ended up hanging out with him a few weeks later at Applebee's, where I was once again with my friends. This time Veronica and her friend joined us in the already-tight booth, and I remember him blowing his nose and leaving the dirty tissue on the table. Then he drove both of us somewhere (Around the block? To the movies? I seem to have blocked out this part of the evening). I went from being impressed to quickly realizing it was his father's old BMW, and it was a stick shift. The five-minute car ride felt like we were riding a bronco, and that is when I realized I wasn't going to marry this tall, hockey-playing BMW owner, although he did smell good. Cologne was his strong point. So I went out with him. Years later, I opened the newspaper, stumbled across his engagement announcement, and had a flashback to our awkward encounters.

Then junior and senior prom came, and before I knew it, graduation was in the nearby future. Aunt Jo took me to get my fake nails, and I made my hair appointment at the salon I always went to. Then that dreaded conversation happened. I asked Sierra whether her boyfriend had any friends I could go to the dance with.

Sierra worked her magic, and by the end of the week, her boyfriend had somebody for me. Sierra gave the guy my screen name and told him to reach out to me. Oh, he did, all right. His name was Kevin, and we chatted a little bit on the computer before he suggested meeting up in person. I told him I would be working at the bagel shop all weekend so he could stop by and we could talk there.

He came in close to two o'clock in the afternoon, when the long lines had died down and my biggest concern wasn't toasting a sesame bagel; it was cleaning the store down with bleach so I could leave on time. He walked over to my coworker. "Are you Katrina?" he whispered across the counter, as if he were a drug dealer. She said no and pointed to me. I took one look at him and immediately wanted to punch Sierra's jerky boyfriend in the face. He looked just like my cousin Ant, because we all want to slow dance and make out in dark parking lots with our cousins.

He was shorter than Ant, but nonetheless, he looked like him. He seemed pleasant enough, and I offered to make him a sandwich since he had come all the way across town to the bagel shop. Of course, he ordered some exotic sandwich on the menu I had neither heard of nor assembled in my year of working there. I had my coworker Tommy make it, while Kevin said, "I thought you said you made the sandwiches." I ignored that and rang him up; then he left.

I ran into our windowless bathroom at work to call Sierra and tell her about him. "What do you mean, he looks like Ant?" she yelled into the phone. Then the countdown to the dance began.

I left school early the day of the junior prom and got my hair done side by side with Veronica at the salon in town while my mom snapped pictures of us. Veronica went home to get ready while my mom helped put my jewelry on and Lin watched me get glamorous. I took photos by the fireplace, posing at various angles. Then the doorbell rang. Kevin was the only one out of us who drove (I felt so cool!), so he picked up Sierra and her boyfriend and brought them to my house for pre-prom pictures.

I distinctly remember Kevin handing me a wad of bills in the doorway of my house. "This is to cover the cost of our tickets to the prom—you keep it," he said, grinning shyly.

"No, no, no, it's my treat. You don't even go to my school and are my date, so I will treat," I said, while my dad grinned from ear to ear behind me. He was the one who said I was not to accept money from the guy under any circumstances, since he was driving me and taking me to a dance at my school. Yet Kevin insisted I take the ninety dollars.

"I've worked some extra shifts at Applebee's lately! They have me working as assistant manager these days," he proudly revealed. So I took the wad of bills from him, and then we all proceeded onto the fireplace to take group pictures. I think my whole family came out to watch my mom take pictures of us. When that fun was over, we hopped in the car, and my dad told us to have fun and for Kevin not to drive like a total ass. Then we went to our friend Ashley's house for more pictures. And guess who happened to be included in this photo session? The guy I'd been in love with in middle school. As if life just couldn't get any more awkward.

When the paparazzi part of the evening was complete, we piled back into Kevin's car to head to the dance. The room was jazzed up, and it was complete with cocktail hour first. As we made our way into the main dining room, Kevin apparently locked eyes with my tall friend Macy. She was sitting at our table and had no date. After heading to the buffet line, Kevin and I tried making small talk about the future.

"Where do you see yourself going to college?" I asked.

He replied, "Somewhere far."

I responded that I would like to go an hour away but no more than that, since I liked seeing my family. He didn't enjoy his family, hence the desire to go far and never look back. We slow danced to one song, despite not really wanting to. We fake-smiled for the camera next to Veronica and her twenty-year-old date, who moonlighted as a DJ.

Then it happened. We went back to the table, and my dateless friend Macy was sitting there, twiddling her thumbs. Kevin asked whether I wanted to slow dance again, and I shook my head, so he asked whether I minded if he asked Macy—you know, since she was alone and all.

Excuse me? I was flabbergasted. But I said, "Okay, sure, why not?" And I sat at the table with all my other single friends watching my date slow dance with my friend. *At my junior prom.* Because that happens all the time, you know.

As you can imagine, I didn't marry Kevin, let alone really ever speak to him again. That May, however, was a friend's birthday, and we went to Applebee's after bowling to celebrate. Lo and behold, guess who was working that night? I snuck into the hallway and asked him whether he could arrange for the waiters to sing to my friend when her dessert came out. He did more than that; he gave us a huge discount on our bill, and we had about five people there. Maybe he wasn't such a bad guy after all.

The following year (senior year) it was all about the prom. I grew up spending countless Saturday nights leafing through Ant's high school yearbooks. I studied the faces of the popular girls, with their fake nails, poufy dresses, and painted-on faces. They all had gorgeous guys on their arms, guys who couldn't wait to spring for a limo and take them to the grand ball. I had imagined this night for many years.

As my high school classmates asked each other out, I wondered whether I should even go. But I loved getting dressed up and envisioned some gorgeous guy sweeping me off my feet and begging me to go with him and make him the happiest guy alive. February rolled around, and still I had no date.

My friend Ricardo worshipped the ground I walked on, and before he came out as gay, he always used to ask me out. So I texted him at the end of language arts: "If we don't have dates to prom, let's go together." And before I knew it, Veronica found me in the halls and cornered me.

"What happened to waiting for Mr. Right to ask you to the prom?" she yelled, apparently already in the know about my text of five minutes earlier.

"Oh please. No one likes me and is ever going to ask me out. Ricardo is a great dancer, and we are close friends, so he and I will go and have a good time."

And we did. The first thing he said to me when he walked in my house the night of prom was, "Oh my God! You have lost so much weight!" and kept saying how beautiful I looked throughout the night. Then, as the evening went on and I watched all the couples around me slow dance, I sulked at the table and cursed being single.

"Katrina, why so sad?" Veronica asked.

I pouted and said I wished I had a boyfriend. Turns out, I wouldn't have a boyfriend for two more years.

I remember reading an article about romance in *Time* magazine when I was in high school, and one of the girls interviewed said she didn't get her first kiss until age eighteen. "What a loser!" I said to Rachel. Well, lo and behold, I would go on to never even hold hands or kiss a guy until I was twenty-two.

When college rolled around, I thought I had it made. There were tons of guys throughout the campus to choose from. I was a four-year college athlete, so I moved into the dorm early and remember Sierra coming to visit one day after pre-season practice. I took her to eat dinner with me in the cafeteria, and as we walked in, we suddenly realized we were the only females in the place. The entire football team was eating and decided to pound their fists on the table and chant as we walked in. I turned beat red but managed to smile as Sierra loved every minute of it.

I did, however, meet a guy in my psychology class who was dark and handsome (not tall, though). He lived in a town next to where I'd grown up and went to all the same places I did. He had an ethnic name and smoked outside before class began, but I wanted him badly. He apparently wanted me too, since he told my tennis teammate that I was "hot." In college, everyone uses the term *hot*. But to me, that was enough to make me think I would have a boyfriend by the time Thanksgiving break rolled around. I used to talk to this guy, and we even studied together once in a group, but then I wised up and forgot him.

As my freshman year moved along, the only man to enter my dorm room was the campus handyman, when the heat broke on the coldest night in January. By the time spring arrived, I was so desperate for a boyfriend that I convinced myself that I liked this long-haired, punk-rock-loving boy, Melvin, in my dorm. He wore tight jeans with a belt and had bracelets that went all up his arm. If you had seen him from the back, you would have thought he was a woman and wonder what type of workout she did to fit into such tight jeans. We had no classes together, but we had some mutual friends, so there were conversation topics. The more we talked, I realized he was sort of funny, and I was convinced he was going to be my first "real" boyfriend.

We started eating dinner in the cafeteria together once or twice a week, and my one friend warned me to "be careful; he looks wild." I invited him to the gym with me one day, and as we were both on the elliptical, he fell off. He literally tumbled onto the floor. I didn't know whether to giggle or scream, so I did both. He was fine, and it was then that I realized he wasn't the athletic type. That disappointed me, but I enjoyed his company and was willing to look past his lack of athleticism.

That never happened, because a few weeks later, on the day we were supposed to meet outside the student center for lunch, he never appeared. I texted him and received no response, so I called him. Nothing. I ended up foregoing lunch altogether and knocking on his dorm door. He answered and was in a strange mood. And the room smelled strange. He invited me in, and I laughed nervously and asked whether he had forgotten to meet me for lunch.

He acted goofy and kept laughing, and I was eighteen and naive, so had no idea what was wrong with him. He was as high as a kite; that's what was wrong with him. I later figured this out after talking to some of the girls in my hallway who knew him. Apparently he got "baked" quite often. I left his room, only to discover vomit on the carpeted hallway floor. Apparently Thirsty Thursday was in full effect by noon.

I didn't know what to do. I felt like I had been punched in the stomach. I liked him, but he'd blown off our lunch date to smoke in his dorm room? I felt sick.

As I walked down the third-floor steps, I decided to stop off at my friend's room on the second floor. I needed someone to talk to. My friends Katie and Angelica opened their room and listened to me tell my story, which started off with, "Hey guys, can I talk to you about something?" They were both sitting on their beds in sweatpants, and they listened as I spoke about how disappointed I was—disappointed because this long-haired crush of mine was a druggie; disappointed because he'd ditched me for lunch and could have cared less. And I was just disappointed because I'd thought my one shot at finally having a boyfriend was happening, when, in fact, I couldn't have felt more sorry for myself. Here I was, having lost forty pounds; and for the first time in my life, I was thin and in great physical shape, yet still no one wanted me. I was alone and would be single forever.

Freshman year came and went, and I was 0–0 in the love department. There was no summer romance. No guys were even really talking to me, if we want to be brutally honest. My interaction with the opposite sex was quite limited. I liked guys; they just never liked me back. When I was heavy, it was obvious why they didn't like me, but here I was, in a brand-new body, and I still was receiving very little attention.

Sophomore year came, and I received more attention but in creepy ways. A tennis teammate of mine had grown up with a guy she thought I might like. I met him one night after she and I went out to dinner; he proceeded to take my number out of her phone and soon began texting and calling me.

I wasn't used to guys communicating with me, so this was hard to handle. I answered on occasion and chatted with him, since he was very nice. Physically he wasn't my type. He was tall, heavyset, and looked very Italian with jet-black hair. He liked to rock a leather jacket too, which reminded me of a Mafia man. He was a nice guy, but I didn't feel sparks, and I didn't know how to turn him off.

One day he called to see whether I wanted to hang out with him that weekend, and he offered to come to the university and pick me up. He lived only ten minutes from campus, and he thought we could see a movie or go out to eat. I was sick and in bed with soup and my pajamas on by five o'clock in the afternoon.

I told him I was feeling under the weather and that it wasn't a good night for a date. He jokingly said he would bring me chicken noodle soup, to which I replied that I already had some, "but thank you anyway." I hung up, and shortly after that, I got a text from him, instructing me to look outside my window. He knew my room was on the first floor (overlooking the tennis courts) because my tennis teammate had told him. I turned around in my bed, pushed aside the blinds, and there he was, standing far away (thank God) but on the street by his car.

He texted, saying that he'd brought me chicken noodle soup. I was as sick as a dog; I'd skipped tennis practice and really wanted to be *left the hell alone.* I ducked beneath the blinds before he had a chance to see me, but he was still a ways away from the window. I texted him, saying how awful I felt and that I really wanted to just take it easy that night. Eventually (after a few more attempts) he got the message, and that was the end of him. I felt bad (as I always do), but I just didn't like him, and although the chicken noodle soup ordeal was very sweet, it came off as too much.

A few more creepy people came knocking on my door, so to speak, but I learned my lesson quicker this time. I wanted a boyfriend, but at the same time, I was doing okay on my own. Then in December Lin's Girl Scout troop had a trip to see *Annie* on Broadway, and my mom bought tickets for the three of us.

Just as my mom was picking me up that Friday night to head home for the show, my suite mate was getting dolled up to go to Rutgers. We were members of the Italian-American club at school, and a few of the senior club leaders were heading to Rutgers for an event with their Italian club. I was invited but couldn't go due to the *Annie* tickets. While I complained to my mom on the bus into the city about how tight my khaki pants were getting, due to a recent weight gain, my suite mate met her future husband. She would come bouncing into my room that Sunday night when I returned to the dorm, practically singing about how she'd met her Prince Charming.

This guy lived forty-five minutes from campus and an hour and a half from her hometown. She was an only child and went home every single weekend, so as you can imagine, that stopped real fast. She now began spending her weekends on campus, with her older boyfriend taking her out to restaurants in town, while I babysat every Saturday night and wished I had the suite to myself on Sundays to do laundry and watch TV all day alone. Before she started staying on campus all weekend, I spent every weekend virtually alone. And I loved it. I seriously did. I worked out each day for an hour, did laundry (and didn't have to fight for a machine due to crowds), got plenty of homework done, and watched TV—all in total silence because all three of my suite mates went home every weekend like clockwork.

Now I had to share my common area with her and her boyfriend. He was pleasant, but he was twenty-four while we were nineteen, yet he wore Scooby-Doo pajamas and called her names like "Honey Bear." I was no longer jealous.

Sophomore year came to a close, and I had a few weeks before my summer job started, so I spent some time at Kelly's house, babysitting her four children. She lived thirty minutes away, very close to New York City, and I was too nervous to drive to her house due to traffic, so she picked me up, and I stayed for a few days at a time. It was a few days before my twentieth birthday, and her oldest daughter, Ariella, had a chorus concert at her elementary school one evening during my stay.

I had just gotten my hair cut the day before, and my hair was still in that shiny, straight phase from the blowout I'd received. We arrived at the concert late, but my cousin's friend had saved us seats, so we were able to slide right in and not cause a scene. I noticed her friend had many children; there seemed to be four little ones sitting in the row and another one on stage. A boy close to my age was also sitting there, and he looked exactly like the children. I nudged my cousin and asked whether all the children were hers, and she said yes. I asked, "Even the older boy?" She said no; that was her friend's brother, Mark, who was staying with them for the summer.

"Why? Do you think he is cute?" she whispered, and I just nodded and kept my eyes focused on the stage.

In the meantime, Ariella was smiling as big as she could, and I could tell she was happy to have me in the audience. During intermission Kelly introduced me to her friend, and I tried to focus on anything but her attractive brother sitting right there. I certainly was interested. Well, the next thing I knew, Kelly told her, "She thinks your brother is hot," while I sat there in my white, glittery Guess T-shirt and Michael Kors jean capris, with my fancy haircut. Let's not forget that blowout.

I looked hot that night, but when I heard that comment, I immediately felt my body temperature become physically hot. My brow turned wet; armpits and hands were suddenly sticky as my body went into full shut-down mode. Instead of being as cool as a cucumber, I was now as hot as a tamale. Then I heard it.

"He thinks you're hot too!" Kelly said. Someone could have told me I had just won the lottery that night, and I could have cared less. All that mattered at the moment in my nineteen-year-old life was that this guy thought I was hot.

The night went on, and Kelly's friend and her brother, Mark, took pictures outside of all the children. Her friend had five children, and they were around the same ages as my cousins, so everyone was chatting and playing with one another as he and I acted like we hadn't just said we thought the other person was hot. I would have been happy just staying in that elementary school parking lot all night long, watching him take photos of his nieces and nephews and hoping he would say I was hot again. Or at least speak to me. But alas, the night was over, and back to Kelly's we went.

As I lay upstairs with Ariella and her younger sister, Marisa, waiting for them to fall asleep so I could tiptoe out and go downstairs to the pullout couch, I looked over, and out their window I could perfectly see the New York City skyline. It was still fairly light out, as it was late spring, and the nights were getting longer as a warm breeze began to fill the New Jersey air. The view was breathtaking, and I remember thinking I was about to have a great summer as I smiled to myself. Turns out, I was right.

The next day I asked a million questions about Mark after we sent the girls off to school. "What is he doing here for the summer? Where does he live? How old is he?" Kelly spit out answers while the two younger babies, Giancarlo and Laila, spit out their food. "He is helping her this summer to babysit all the kids. He is from Sacramento, where his sister lived before her husband had a job transfer. He is eighteen."

I was a little bummed out about his age, as I was about to turn twenty in two weeks, but other than that, he intrigued me. His sister called Kelly to chat around noon and casually mentioned that she, Mark, and the three younger children were going to Starbucks and to run some errands. Would I like to join them? I welcomed this opportunity to escape for a short while.

I was told to be ready, and she would swing by in her minivan in about twenty minutes. I hadn't packed makeup or much jewelry with me, since the only people I expected to see during my trip were children. I put on the T-shirt and jean capris I'd packed for that day, borrowed some of Kelly's perfume, and was out the door.

I was nervous but also excited. I sat in the backseat with the babies, while Mark sat in the front seat. He barely acknowledged my presence when I climbed into the vehicle, and as she went through the Starbucks drive-through, his response was essentially the same thing. I ordered a Frappuccino and offered to pay, but she insisted it was her treat. Then we went shopping, and he continued to ignore me. He smiled and listened when I talked to his sister, but basically he was silent. I wasn't nearly as chatty back then as I am now, so I just went with the flow. When the day was over and it was time to return to craziness, I was sad that he hadn't asked me out. Or talked to me.

But just as I was giving Kelly a play-by-play of the day, her cell phone rang, and it was his sister. Without even saying hello, she picked up and said, "So does he think she is hot or what?" And to my horror, it was Mark who had stolen her phone to ask Kelly for my phone number. I could have died right there. Yup, just take me out back and shoot me. As Kelly rattled off my cell phone number and said, "Well, thanks for calling, Mark, and tell your sister I will call her later," I was now jumping for joy. I was going on a date!

I remember him calling me that night, and we talked for an hour in my walk-in closet at home. Well, *I* was in my closet, since I like to make all my private and important phone calls from there. We laughed and talked about what he thought about New Jersey, and then he asked when my next trip to Kelly's was. Although it hadn't been confirmed, my next trip would be the following week, when I wasn't working at the Y for a few days.

The following week we texted, and he asked whether I wanted to go with him to the Meadowlands Fair, which is a huge deal in New Jersey. Kelly dropped us off, and he walked up to the ticket booth to buy two tickets, while I remained silent but was smiling on the inside. I thanked him and offered to pay him back as we walked away from the booth and into the fair, but he insisted that wasn't necessary. I was so awkward and wouldn't eat anything, and I silently prayed that he wouldn't get hungry and want food either. I was too worried about looking like a pig or having food in my teeth, so I instead pretended that I had no appetite whatsoever. We walked slowly through the fair, taking it all in.

When I saw a booth for "The World's Smallest Woman!" and was interested in going in, he paid for us both, and we went in. When he asked whether I wanted to play a game, he paid for us both and won me a prize. When I finally realized my stomach was growling and I no longer could play the "I'm not hungry" game anymore, I broke down and let him buy me a cup of peanut butter frozen yogurt. I was a late bloomer, but I was starting to understand that this was what it felt like to really like someone—and have the person like you back.

The fair ended with his sister picking us up. I felt safe with the fact that my cousin and his sister were picking us up and dropping us off; that way there were no awkward kissing moments or hugs where one person sticks out his or her ass as a way to avoid coming too close. He didn't have a car and was only staying the summer, and I didn't feel comfortable driving to that area, so we made do.

Our next date consisted of my walking over with Ariella and Marisa for a play date with his nieces and nephews. His sister was in the kitchen, washing and cutting up bell peppers and arranging them on a plate with hummus, which I had never tried before. She offered me a sandwich while the kids ran throughout the house playing. I once again was too nervous to gnaw on a huge sandwich in front of her hot brother, but I was pretty hungry. To my luck, he excused himself and went upstairs to the bedrooms—and never came back.

What I had thought was a quick bathroom run turned out to be a nap. Very odd, I know. I later came to realize that his sister and her husband often left him to babysit all five of the children while they went out to go house shopping or to do errands, so he was exhausted most of the time. I now had no problem eating an entire sandwich, since I knew he was napping. She then began to do scrapbooking, and I realized their entire family was very much into photography, since many of the pictures were of Mark holding one of the children by the beach. But instead of being dressed in sandals and a muscle T-shirt, he was dressed in a nice button-down shirt and pants. They went to places such as the shore or a park and posed for pictures there, instead of just taking them at JCPenney with fake smiles. "Can I have ...," I started to say as I touched the photographs gently on the table.

"Of course! I was once a young girl myself," she said as she winked at me.

I still have those five photos in a box beneath my bed. There is one of Mark and his baby niece, and the rest are of him down on the shore.

Mark and I continued to talk on the phone, and each week I went down to Kelly's to babysit for a few days and see Mark. Our next visit was interesting, and I still can feel myself getting red in the face thinking about it. It was the Saturday of Chrissy's high school graduation party, and afterward I was going back with Kelly to stay over. I wore a cute sundress and dressy sandals, and I had done my hair all nice and curly for the party.

When we got back to Kelly's, Mark invited Ariella, Marisa, and me over to the game room in his condo complex to watch a movie. He brought his two nieces and nephew, and all five of the children were loud and excited to see each other. The room was small, with two sets of brand-new couches in two rows and the large television and DVD player mounted on the wall. He popped in the movie and had made popcorn beforehand, so we sat on the couch in front of the children, and he munched away.

We sat about a foot apart, making sure no body parts were touching in any way, shape, or form. But then I heard it, the giggling coming from the children behind us. I tried to tune them out and kept telling myself to focus on the movie, but it became rather difficult to do so when popcorn began hitting me in the back of the head.

Mark must have been trying his best to tune them out as well, but he finally snapped. He jerked his head around and yelled, "What are you doing? Watch the movie and be quiet!" He turned back around, all red in the face. Moments later, the giggling and popcorn throwing began again. Now it was my turn to turn around, and of course, when I yelled at my cousins, they blamed it on his family members. "But they started it!" is what I heard.

We paused the movie, and Mark said he wouldn't resume it until they cut the crap or so to speak. Then my worst nightmare came true. "Kiss her! Kiss her!" they began to chant, all five of them practically in song.

I wanted the sofa to open up and swallow me whole. I kept hissing for them to stop it, but my cries fell on deaf ears. Mark kept telling them to stop it as well, before giving up and bending over to hit the "play" button on the DVD player. This time I could feel eyes on me and felt them basically breathing down my neck as I glanced over my shoulder.

"What are you doing? Go sit on your couch!" I yelled.

"Mark, can you please kiss her? *Please*?" his older niece squealed. "Can you marry Katrina? I want Ariella to be my sister!" Imagine all this before the guy had even asked me to be his official girlfriend. When all five of the children began to chant again for him to kiss me, he finally said, "I ate onions before, so I can't. Oh well!" as a way to get them to shut up.

It was pretty funny on his part, and they quieted down for a few moments before asking whether we were going to get married again. I was dying on the inside and once again felt myself get very hot on the outside, on this already-hot summer night in July 2007. The movie ended, and he dropped off his three small family members and then walked my two and me back to Kelly's. There was no kiss in the moonlight or ass-out hug. Just a simple, "I will talk to you tomorrow—good night" And he turned to walk home. I was more than fine with that. My nerves couldn't handle a kiss or hug just yet.

The following night Mark texted, asking whether I wanted to come by and watch a movie in the game room … alone. I was nervous and ecstatic at the same time. I really liked him, and the fact that he was so cute was a turn-on. Kelly dropped me off and said to make sure he walked me home at night when the movie was over, and if he wanted to come back to her place after that to hang with me, that was okay. I don't even remember what movie we watched that night, but I remember us sitting about five feet apart, and I kept worrying whether my breath smelled, my skin looked greasy, or I had food in my teeth from the imaginary food I consumed as we watched the movie.

We sat in silence, watching the movie, and then he walked me back, and I invited him to watch another movie at Kelly's. All the kids were sleeping, and she made us popcorn and went to read magazines in bed while she waited for her husband to come home. When he strolled in, the first thing he saw when he reached the top of the staircase was Mark and me on his sofa; we were rolling around as we made out.

I'm totally kidding. We were once again sitting five feet apart, with the popcorn bowl in between us. "Oh, hey there! Is, uh, Kelly home?" he asked. I said, yes, of course, that she was in the bedroom reading. He left us to watch the remainder of the movie, and then I said good night, and Mark walked home. There was still no hug, hand holding, or kiss.

We were in the car the week afterward with his sister when we dropped him off at work. As she drove us back in silence, she jokingly asked whether he had kissed me yet. I was used to fielding these questions from Kelly, so I said no. She laughed but said he probably wouldn't kiss me until we were engaged. Umm, what?

Then it all seemed to make sense. His family was very religious. All the women in his family had abnormally long hair. They wore no makeup, and they weren't allowed to paint their nails or wear jewelry. The one time I'd painted his young niece's nails, his brother-in-law had walked by and said they looked pretty but were inappropriate. They were big on home schooling, and when his sister had become pregnant, she didn't go to a doctor for most of the pregnancy, saying she "knew what she was doing." As you can imagine, my family didn't approve or agree with this lifestyle. They were nice people who welcomed me with open arms, but I didn't know where the relationship was going to go.

Later that summer, Kelly moved to a new house, which was an hour away, and she no longer was down the block from Mark and his family. One warm summer night, he asked whether I wanted to come down and go bowling. I was too nervous at the thought of driving there alone, so I enlisted a former best friend of mine to come. We both loved bowling and went frequently, so we were quite excited. We got to his sister's place, and somehow or other, the children ended up tagging along—not all of them, just the three older ones. His sister offered to drop us off at the bowling alley and pick us up.

Now, it was a weeknight, and while I worked only part-time in child care during the summer, my friend had an internship. When we were just about done bowling, he went to call his sister to pick us up. No answer. He tried again and again, and he just kept going to her voice mail on her cell phone. I suggested he call the house line, to which he replied, "We don't have one." *Great.*

He tried his brother-in-law's cell phone, and there was no answer there either. I went from panicking to being aggravated. Shortly after that, she pulled into the parking lot at ten thirty. On a Wednesday night. When she knew it was way past the bedtimes of her three children, all below the age of ten.

My friend was a nervous wreck and kept calling her mom. For what, I'm not exactly sure. It was summer, and it was time to live a little. But her mom was disappointed, and my friend was panicked. By the time we got back to my house, it was close to midnight, and my friend raced home, since she had to leave for work early in the morning. My mom was disappointed too, but the way I look at it was, it was one summer night when we stayed out a little too late. So what? So you are tired for work one time. Her internship was fifteen minutes from her house. I was very annoyed with his sister's lackluster attitude and was having doubts about how his family behaved.

As summer wrapped up, Mark's mother was due to spend two weeks with them. I was nervous to meet her, but when I did, I found her to be sweet. She spoke broken English, but one of the first things she said to me was, "Mark never told me how beautiful you are. Wait until I call my husband and tell him." And she then proceeded to do so.

I was invited to sleep over, and I distinctly remember standing in my kitchen with my duffel bag when my dad asked me where I would be sleeping. "With his two nieces, in their room," I said.

He replied, "Make sure of it. No funny business." I still cringe when I think back to that moment and think perhaps maybe at age twenty I was too young to be sleeping over at a boy's family's house. I had a fun time with his family, and his sister even asked me whether I wanted to drive back with them to California to drop off the mom. It turns out that they thought a one-way plane ticket was too much money, so instead they thought they would pack up all the children and Mark, and just drive her back to California. Just like that. They were even going to leave two days earlier then scheduled to "surprise" Mark's two sisters, who were manning the fort while their mom was in New Jersey. While I had always dreamed of taking a road trip from here to California, I was due to move back into the dorms during the time they were going. I moved into the dorms a week earlier than everyone else due to playing tennis, and besides, classes would be starting up, and I needed to buy my books and prepare for my junior year.

Off they went. His sister drove the entire time, stopping only for coffee, gas, and bathroom breaks. Mark took beautiful pictures out the window, documenting the trip as they went. I especially liked one of a pink sky at sunrise somewhere in the Nevada desert. While he was away, he called me once, texted me daily, and sent me a postcard, saying he was having fun with friends but missed me.

While he was gone, my mom decided to have a chat with me about Mark. She caught me right as I was leaving the kitchen and walking up the side staircase to my room. "I want to talk to you about this little relationship of yours" is how she phrased it. "What exactly is going on with you and this boy? His family doesn't seem to know if they are going or coming. Are they staying here or going back to California?"

I was so upset that I started to cry. He was the first boy I had every liked, and she was basically telling me to dump him. I defended him the best I could and then stormed upstairs. I overheard my dad come into the kitchen and ask why I was so upset, and she whispered and told him, while I quietly listened in from the balcony upstairs. Looking back, she had a point. His family was far from normal, they had nothing in common with the way we (or most of society) lived life, and he really didn't know whether he was going or coming. Mark came back from his trip two weeks later and was refreshed after having spent time camping and fishing with his father.

I didn't have class on Wednesdays that year, so his sister brought him and the kids by to see my campus and dorm. After Mark's family left, he met my roommate, Callie (who said he was "so hot"); then I gave him a tour of my campus, and we walked into town and got ice cream before it was time for him to take a train back. We should have gotten dinner, but once again, I still wouldn't really eat in front of him, so ice cream had to cut it. As the day got shorter and the summer weather began to fade, we sat smiling at each other and eating our ice creams, as we waited for his train to pull up. I figured out that he would have to switch once, but the ride in total was only about forty minutes and cost maybe ten bucks. He wasn't even from this state yet the thought of switching trains in unfamiliar towns didn't faze him.

He showed no signs of being nervous. He was confident, and I knew he would find his way back. As the train pulled up and screeched to a halt, I wondered whether he would give me a romantic kiss as I saw him off. He gave me an ass-out hug instead and said he would "text me later."

Callie picked me up at the station and asked how my day with Mark had been. "Fabulous. Simply fabulous." I beamed.

The following Sunday I stayed on campus and didn't have much planned, so I suggested to Mark that I take the train to him and spend the day with his family. I was giddy as the train pulled in, and I mastered the switching part, so I was just happy I had gotten there in one piece. We ended up walking to the train again later on and going into the city. He was only one stop away, and the ride cost something ridiculous, like $2.50 one way. It was foolish *not* to go into the city at least once.

We posed for a photo in Central Park, and he bought me my very first apron in the M&M store in Times Square. I was so nervous to be in a picture with him, so my eyes were shut, but the backdrop was beautiful. He was pretty hungry, but I didn't want to eat in front of him (I was still too worried about food in my teeth ... after knowing him for four months now), so he got pizza to go and ate it as we walked.

I felt awful but didn't know what else to do. I'd eaten nothing all day; I'd just sipped my water bottle and said I was fine. When we got back to his house, his sister was making a Sunday night dinner of meatballs and spaghetti. I was famished, and my feet were killing me from walking in the city all day, so I slid off my purple-jeweled flip-flops and sat down at the table with the kids. He went upstairs ... and never came back down. I assumed he was going to the bathroom, so we waited for him, but then his sister instructed me to just dig in, so I did. He never came down. It turned out he was taking a nap upstairs. It was awfully strange not to tell your family or "girlfriend" that.

His sister asked whether I wanted any leftovers to take back with me, and I was overjoyed at the thought of having real food in my tiny dorm fridge, so I said yes; that would be great. I still have the one container she gave me with the leftovers; each time I use it for my work lunches, I have a flashback to that Sunday night, even if it lasts only a second. When Mark finally showed his face, it was time to walk me back to the train station. It was seven o'clock and dark out, so I was glad to have him walk me back. His youngest nephew begged to go with "Uncle Mark" when he took me back to the train station and carried on so much that Mark agreed.

I gathered my belongings, thanked his sister again for the nice dinner, and hugged the children. We got to the train station, and he knew I had to switch at the first stop but bought a ticket for himself because he didn't want me to wait alone at night. He never directly said so, but just by his quietly buying his own ticket, I knew what he was doing. His little nephew got to ride for free and was tickled to be onboard the train. We were waiting in the station for our trains to pull up (his to go back, mine to take me near campus) when the screen showed that his train would arrive ten minutes before mine. I went down the staircase to wait for my train and hugged him good-bye, since his was due to pull in any minute. Two minutes later, I looked over, and the scene was literally something out of a movie; Mark smiled and walked towards me, his nephew by his side.

"What are you doing here? Did you miss your train?" I asked him, with my eyes wide and worried.

"Yes, but it's okay. I didn't want you waiting down here by yourself," he said, and I beamed from ear to ear. He'd purposely missed his train so he could wait with me.

The next week was busy with my first home tennis match of the season that Friday night and classes in full swing. Mark said he was going to send me a gift to help me get through the week, and I joked and said, "Sure you are." But when I went to my mailbox later that week, there was a tiny note inside, instructing me to head to the mailroom on campus to pick up a package. A large box awaited me, with a Vermont Teddy Bear inside. Mark had ordered me a tennis bear engraved with my name on it. Kelly had gotten a wedding bear as a gift when she got married, so I knew these dolls were costly. He was a man of a few words, so the card simply said, "Hey, I told you I would send you something today," and yes, indeed, he did. I was over the moon and showed the bear off to all my friends. At age twenty, I was finally receiving stuffed animals from guys, when most of my friends had received them back in middle school or high school.

The weeks in September flew by, and I was busy in my clubs and playing tennis every day after class. I texted and called Mark and saw him once a week, but then he announced he was heading back to California. He said he wasn't sure whether his relocating was permanent or not, but his parents missed him, and he wanted to apply for jobs out there. I was upset but remember thinking everything over; and then the next day, I told him we "should talk." Basically over the phone we decided that since he was heading back, we should break up, but we could always keep in touch. I remember being sad and texting my best friend, "I will never find anyone ever again," and she told me to be quiet and that of course I would.

Kelly called me two months later and said Mark had joined the Marines and was leaving for Japan soon. I was shocked; he'd never mentioned he was interested in joining the services, but I didn't think college was in the cards for him. She told me to call him and wish him well in case, God forbid, something should happen to him. I was nervous on the phone and told him to be careful. He said the training would be lengthy and that he wasn't sure when he would have his phone. Then off he went.

I didn't hear from Mark until that February after my dad passed away. He was back from Japan and called me when he heard the news from his sister. I didn't have his number in my phone anymore, but when I heard the voice, my pulse sped up. I gave him some of the details of what was going on and thanked him for calling. Then he texted me, "I am so sorry about what happened to your dad. If I ever did anything to ever hurt you, Katrina, I am very sorry and hope you can one day forgive me. I enjoyed our time together so much this past summer and hope I was never a jerk to you. You are a wonderful person, and I loved spending time with you."

I was speechless. I wrote back that no, he had never done anything to hurt me and that I'd loved our time together too. We probably could have gotten married and been on our way to having seven children by now, but he was moving back across the country, and I had a very active life back in New Jersey, one I had no plan to give up.

The year went on, and his sister and her family left New Jersey and moved to Pennsylvania, to a town an hour away from me. I had been to that area a few times, and it was pretty quiet but had a huge outlet shopping center I liked. I saw pictures, and the house was beautiful, sitting on acres of land.

During the first week in May, my phone buzzed while I was in class, and it was you-know-who. He was staying with his sister for the week and asked whether I wanted to come up and visit. I was in the middle of final exams. He didn't get it. I had to finish up exams and then pack up my entire dorm to move home for the summer, so no, I didn't have time to drive over an hour to Pennsylvania to see him. I wasn't the type to drive far either, so that also was a reason not to go. I don't even think I texted him back.

Summer came and then fall, and I forgot all about him. No one else asked me out, although this one boy from college, who is now a doctor, told me I was "very pretty," but that was it. Then December rolled around, and I was out with my coworker and gym buddy, Alexa, when a text rolled in. It was the night of the YMCA's annual employee holiday party, and we were dolled up, dancing at a fancy country club nearby. She left to get a drink, and I happened to check my phone, when I stopped short. She appeared and asked who it was, and I said it was Mark. He wished me a merry Christmas and said he was off to training again soon, but this time it was in San Diego. He would be gone for about six months, and training was going to be intense. We keep texting as the days went on. Then at Kelly's for Christmas Eve he texted me a picture of all the kids and him lined up by their tree, and I showed my cousins. We texted back and forth until he left for San Diego, and then that was that.

After Mark, I told my friends I would be single forever and never find anyone ever again. But that was fine because I wasn't really seeking or asking for it. It didn't exactly cross my mind, because I had so much going on in my life after college. Then love struck, and it hit me like a thunderbolt.

I can remember the day I first heard about Jack like it was yesterday. I was on a cruise with my family (the first year without my dad), and we were stuck in the Miami Airport, since our flight back to New Jersey kept getting delayed due to the weather back home. I was reading trashy magazines when my phone rang, and it was my college friend Angelica. She was one of the first friends I'd met in college upon arrival in the freshman dorms, and she wasn't one for calls—texts and e-mails, yes—so I was surprised when I saw she was calling.

I remember getting up to talk to her, and she said, "Katrina, I want to talk to you about something. I work with this guy, and he reminds me a lot of you. He plays tennis, wants to go on a road trip, has a good family, and is Catholic. I want you two to go out. What do you think?"

I was speechless and said to her, "Ugh, Ang, I don't know. What does he look like?"

"Katrina, he is very cute. And I wouldn't say that if he wasn't. Trust me!"

Still unsure, I asked her where he lived, and she named a town about thirty-five minutes west of me, where a former best friend of my dad lived. I remember going to visit my dad's friend once while growing up and thinking the town was so far away. That already put me on the fence because I didn't like to drive far, and I was already thinking about how I would get there. The final piece of the puzzle came when I asked his age and found out he was two years younger. I didn't know how mature he would be, but Angelica assured me that he was very mature for his age. I thought it couldn't hurt to go out with him, and plus, I felt better having her suggest him. I agreed to let her work her magic, and she said I would hear from him. Well, I didn't.

Weeks rolled by, and as the winter months got colder, I was dying inside. "Why hasn't he texted? Did you give him the right number?" were the questions I spat out at Angelica and her former fiancé each time they were over. One night in particular, during that cold February 2010, she actually shook her head in annoyance in my kitchen and said she was so sorry Jack hadn't reached out to me.

March arrived, and there was still no word from him. Then in early April, I paid a visit to the movie theater where Angelica and Jack worked. Angelica was working there while she searched for a full-time gig, and Jack was in community college at the time, and he lived the town over from the theater. It was an awfully long hike just to see a movie, but Angelica told me I could see a free movie while she worked and have all the free popcorn and soda I wanted. I was sold.

While I don't remember what movie I saw that day, I do remember the day. It was raining, and I got to the theater late (as always). I rushed inside, all dressed up in a long sweater, leggings, and flat boots, because after the movie I was heading to a Japanese restaurant for a reunion with my high school friends; Ricardo was in town after he moved away for a job after college. Angelica had a coworker who apparently was in on the whole "Katrina and Jack setup." While my eyes nervously darted across the counter, wondering whether one of the boys making popcorn or sweeping the floors was him, her coworker asked me, "Does Jack know how pretty you are?"

And another high school girl chimed in with, "Yea, you are really pretty!"

I was flattered and thanked them but knew they were just teasing. I whispered to Angelica, "Is he … here?"

She said, "Who? Jack? Oh no, today is his day off," and I felt my heart rip in half.

As April rolled in, I became increasingly tired of working only part-time and needed a break from the endless days of job searching. I contacted a good friend of mine from college, whose parents divorced after she graduated and her mom and her and her younger siblings moved to South Carolina to start fresh. I asked whether I could come visit, and the idea made her ecstatic. A few other people I knew from college had already gone down to see her, and I knew she was excited about the idea of more company. I met her at Campus Crusade for Christ (a club on campus), and we hit it off immediately; she was fun and friendly, and she had such a nice smile. Whenever my mom came to pick me up on the weekends, she always chatted with her. I was feeling adventurous, booked a round-trip ticket for Amtrak, and waved good-bye to my mom at the station. There I was, on board a train for thirteen hours, and couldn't have been more excited.

While on board, I brought plenty of work with me and began to type away as the scenery around me changed. The waifish woman sitting next to me was silent as I typed, and for a moment, I wished I had the seat all to myself. I had a medium-sized suitcase, my laptop case, a carry-on bag, and my purse. After about an hour on the train, I stopped typing and looked across her, out the window.

"I hope the weather is nicer the farther south we go," I muttered.

She looked out the window and remarked, "I hope so too. Where are you headed?"

I told her I was off to Columbia, South Carolina, and she was too—and it turned out she had been born and raised there. "Your first time there?" she asked.

"No, I went to Hilton Head last spring, but this is my first time headed to Columbia," I replied.

I typed some more, and she asked whether I was in college and was working on homework. I explained that I was a journalist but at the time was doing only freelance and had a few articles to write and submit while I was away. I thought there was no greater time to type than while on board a train for nearly a day. Just as luck would have it, she told me she was a former journalist ... for the *New York Times*.

I almost pissed myself. When I told her rather sheepishly that I worked for a small medical magazine but had been let go after four months due to the economy being bad, she was sympathetic and told me the *New York Times* had let her go due to the same reason. She was headed home to her "favorite place on earth," where she still had a small house and was looking forward to seeing her friends.

After we gabbed away for what seemed like an eternity, she wrote down her name and e-mail address, and told me to reach out when I got home. She also mentioned that a very good friend of hers was the food editor of a popular magazine in the city, and she could easily arrange for us to meet. I was floored—this woman was going out of her way after just meeting me. I texted Mom and Mikey and he said, "The fact she of all people is sitting next to you is a sign from Dad. These chance encounters do not just happen!" and I knew he was right.

She napped, and I continued to type. When she awoke, I mentioned that I was thinking of going to the meal car to get food and asked her to join me. We took our purses and laptops with us and walked through all the cars until we got to the dining car. It was small but had white linen table clothes and real forks and knives. A waiter took our order, and surprisingly there were more meal choices than I had anticipated. I ordered vegetable lasagna, which came with a small salad and a roll with butter. My new friend ordered her meal and glass of wine, which I was impressed to see they offered.

I will never forget eating my microwaved lasagna and watching the sun set over the rolling hills of North Carolina. The sky was a pinkish color, and all the eye could see was farm after farm. I was in a really happy place; I felt safe on board the train and lucky to have such a wonderful new friend seated next to me. I was also excited to see my college friend, and lastly, I was anxious to get back to New Jersey and hopefully have a date with Jack.

After dinner, we retreated back to our seats, and as I typed in the darkness, people all around us fell asleep. I texted my friend to make sure she was awake and ready to pick me up when I arrived at one o'clock in the morning. When my train pulled in, I waved good-bye to my new pal and told her I would "look her up when I got home."

I looked around at the clientele waiting at the station, and I immediately felt my stomach twist into knots. Where was my friend? *God, I hope she didn't fall asleep and forget to come.* The station was very small and old fashioned; it was unlike anything I had ever seen before up north.

I called my friend, and thank God, she was parked out front with her friend, and I was in the back of the station. I walked around and saw her. After exchanging a big hug, her friend tossed my suitcase into his truck, and we headed to her family's condo. I was exhausted from my long day but at the same time curious as to where I was and what this part of the country had to offer. I sneaked peeks out the window as my eyes dozed off.

My next few days in Columbia were fun and relaxing. We slept in, and then my friend drove me around and introduced me to things this Jersey girl had never even thought about, let alone tried. I had my first Krispy Kreme doughnut (hot out of the oven), chicken-fried steak, and more collard greens than you could imagine. We toured the University of South Carolina, shopped in the tree-lined downtown area, and went into a few country stores. The weather was a lot warmer than I anticipated, and I was glad I had packed sandals and gotten a pedicure with my babysitting money before I came down.

We went out one night with her younger sister and friend to a bar that had trivia night and where a ton of the USC kids hung out. We also had lunch in downtown Columbia one day when she had a date. She was worried about meeting this guy off a dating website, and he'd happened to message her the week I was visiting, so she asked whether he minded if I came along, and he didn't. The guy was somewhat attractive and very nice; he bought us both lunch at this very busy lunch spot in town, which was similar to a Panera. I did most of the talking; my friend, who was always unusually chatty, wasn't into him and was awfully quiet. After the date ended, she said he reminded her of her cousin, and that was that. She joked that I should go out with him. That wouldn't be needed, because I received quite a surprise when I logged into my Facebook account that night.

I received a message *and* a friend request from Jack. I accepted it immediately and then read his message. It was very businesslike and something to the effect of, "Hi, Katrina. Angelica has told me about you, and you seem like a great person. I would like the opportunity to get to know you. Would you like to meet up sometime? Sincerely, Jack." Not only was he super polite, but he was cute too. I did what I thought was the "cool thing" and didn't message him back for two days. I thought playing it cool was the best approach; plus I didn't want to seem too eager after he'd waited four months and not used my telephone number.

When I decided to write back, I told him I would love to get together but was currently in South Carolina, so I could meet when I returned. He wrote back on my last day in Columbia, saying that was fine, and he hoped I was enjoying the warm weather, since it was raining back in New Jersey. I called Angelica on my train ride home and told her all about my trip and said I was ecstatic about my date the following week with Jack. She was giddy for me too and told me to make sure I told her all about it afterward.

Jack asked whether I wanted to grab coffee somewhere and suggested a town fifteen minutes away from me. I said that was fine, but then I suggested the town where the movie theater was because it was also a cute, quaint, little town that had a coffee shop. He politely said he would rather come to see me and suggested "getting a bite to eat after," which made me smile because my dad always used that phrase. It was all set up, and I couldn't have been more excited to get back to the Garden State.

My train pulled up that Sunday night at dinnertime, and my mom and Lin were there to greet me and hear all about my awesome trip. I told them all the details as we drove home and mentioned my even bigger news. I had a date next week. Jack asked what night worked for me, and I suggested Friday or Saturday, but he said, "How about Thursday? It's sooner." I was already falling in love with this stranger. I had a lot of work to do, though, in preparation for this big date. I spent that Thursday, April 22, 2010, at a workout class and then rushed home to shower. I had a facial, haircut and blowout, and manicure and pedicure appointment. I spent over $200 to look good for Jack, and I felt like a million bucks.

Some girls buy new outfits for first dates; I choose to get groomed and wear clothes already in my closet. I wore a pair of Lucky Brand jeans, a long-sleeve black Anne Klein shirt, a long necklace, and open-toed black flats with a small wedge. I went into my mom's room to announce I was leaving and asked how I looked. "I feel fat; I should have dieted more before this date!" I wailed, but she told me I looked great.

"Now, where are you going? And show me this guy's picture!" she said, and I told her the Starbucks and said we were going to try this one restaurant in town later. When I showed her his picture, she said, "Oh, he is handsome!"

He offered to pick me up, but I politely declined. After all, I didn't know him yet. And then I saw it was 5:05 p.m., and we were meeting at 5:30, so I rushed out the door and into the warm night while grimacing. The sky looked a little dark and gloomy.

For once in my life, I was the early one. This was exactly how I planned the date to go in my head. I got there without rushing; I found a parking spot and went to the bathroom to check for lipstick stains on my teeth (None. Whew!); then I grabbed a seat. When I saw the clock inch closer to five thirty and he wasn't there yet, I breathed easy and grabbed a copy of the *New York Times* someone had left behind on the table next to me.

Yes, that was perfect. That way when he walked in and saw me reading it, he would think I was really smart. Bingo! Then I got a text message from him: "Hi, Katrina. Angelica gave me your phone number. I am running late but will be there soon." I then realized we never had exchanged phone numbers. We'd just messaged back and forth on Facebook a few times and agreed to meet. He had my number because Angelica had given it to him back in January, but I never got his.

So I sat for a few more minutes, casually tried to read the *New York Times*, and kept telling myself not to get nervous, because when I get nervous, I sweat. A lot. *No one likes sweaty people, Katrina. You spent more than $200 getting groomed today. Get ahold of yourself!* I told myself over and over and watched the door like a hawk, seeing each and every male visitor enter the Starbucks and wondering whether he was Jack. Then an overweight guy, who was about my age, came toward the door, wearing ripped-up sweatpants and looking right at me.

"Oh God, please no. Say it isn't so," I whispered, telling myself that Angelica couldn't be that cruel. Or blind.

Then a few moments passed, and I received a text from Jack, telling me he was wearing a red plaid shirt. The door swung open, and there he was.

He came in, looked around quickly, and then caught my eye. I did the only thing I could think of: I waved him over. He was older looking than I anticipated but I found him to be attractive. I pushed aside the newspapers and casually explained I was just reading while I waited for him. He apologized for being late and said he'd gotten lost, since he didn't come to this area all that much. Then he switched gears and asked how my trip to South Carolina had been, and we avoided all that stupid talk about weather that most first dates naturally drift toward. He was smiling as I told him all about my trip, and then we shifted gears into tennis, and it turned out he was an instructor for a few summers and taught lessons to children.

He was polite, and we had such a good time talking that, before we both knew it, neither one of us had gotten coffee or tea, and almost two hours had passed. He asked whether I wanted to walk downtown a bit, so we did, and I blabbered the whole time about the history of the town (God, I was lame) and pointed out shops and eateries I had been to while silently telling myself to "just shut up!" I remember stepping down off the curb at one point and realizing I was slightly taller than he was with my wedged shoes. I thought to myself that being on the short side was his only downfall.

I picked up the pace until he asked whether I was hungry. Eating food was the last thing I wanted to do. (Remember all my dates with Mark? No food!) But Jack had come all the way from his house, and it was almost eight o'clock by now, so yes, food probably was a good idea. I'd researched the menus of all the places in town earlier that day; therefore, I knew about some "safe" choices to order. (By safe, I of course mean items that wouldn't be too messy and/or get stuck in my front teeth.)

We picked this restaurant/café, and I immediately knew what to order, since I'd spent so much time looking at their menu earlier. I thought it was awfully strange when Jack said to the waiter, "Do you just have grilled chicken?" The waiter said he could do that, but did he want sides? Jack politely said, "No, thank you"; he just wanted the chicken.

So out came our meals; I had very safe chicken in a peanut sauce with brown rice and mixed vegetables, and there was Jack's grilled chicken breasts. We chatted and ate; then he excused himself and headed to the bathroom, and then I did the same. I received a few texts from my mom, and two best friends asked how the date was going. My mom texted, "The date is now going on 4 hours. Should I call the cops?" I had a good chuckle but quickly wrote back that I was fine. Then I hurried out of the bathroom. I didn't want him to think I was pooping in there.

We walked back to the Starbucks parking lot, he hugged me good-bye, and I thanked him for a great night. As we stood in the parking lot that warm April night, he said the ever-so-cliché "Let's do this again soon!" I remember really hoping that he meant it.

I strolled in close to nine thirty, and my mom and Lin wanted to hear all about my date. I called Sierra too and filled her in, and then a few nights later, I called Angelica and gave her every detail. Jack texted me when he got home that night, saying he'd had a great time and that "we should do this again soon!" I wrote back and thanked him for a great night and agreed. And then I didn't hear from him for weeks.

I was confused as hell. Had I made this up in my head? I thought he was charming and intelligent and couldn't wait to go out with him again. Did this date really happen, or had I dreamt it? I tried waiting for him to reach out, but he didn't. So I thought of reasons to text him. A friend's mother got wind of a job fair being held not far from the community college Jack was attending, but I couldn't place where it was, so I texted him to ask. He said he wasn't sure where that place was, and that was it. I had to keep the flame going, so I asked how he was, and he replied that he was busy with finals starting and graduation around the corner.

A few days later, I was on the bus to the city, heading to a meeting with a college acquaintance for a journalism conference we were attending that evening. I had just gotten on the bus when she texted me: "Sorry, not going to make it into the city today. Have way too much to do around the house."

I was floored and terrified at the same time. It was barely two o'clock, and the conference wasn't starting until seven. It was my first time heading to New York City solo, and I didn't know what to do. So I did the only logical thing a girl should do. I texted Jack. I thought by asking him for his recommendations on what to do with my time on this cold, damp spring day, alone in the best city in the world, I would somehow gain insight into how his brain worked. He really had no idea and told me to have fun. *Wow.*

I ended up having a nice time that day. I window-shopped, took in a museum, and ate dinner at my favorite Chinese restaurant (alone with my trusted *New York Times* someone had left behind) before heading to my event in the Hearst Building.

The following Sunday (early May) was Angelica's birthday. She was having a small gathering at our favorite bar/restaurant in our college town. She invited me and said I could invite Jack. I asked him whether he was interested in coming to the birthday dinner, but he said he couldn't; he had too many finals to study for. So I stopped asking.

I felt silly at that point. I moped around my house like a loser, and as I watched *The Bachelor* alone in my living room each week, I wondered whether Jack was ever going to ask me out again. Then he did.

He apologized for not being around much and suggested we get together. He didn't say what we should do, so I suggested mini golf, and we ended up going to a really nice place right by his house. It was a hot afternoon, and we were the only ones there, since it was the middle of the workweek. The whole time we were outside on the bright sunny day, I realized my large, plaid Tommy Hilfiger purse wasn't practical, and I would have rather eaten dirt than put it on the ground each time I went to hit a ball. Jack held my bag each and every time it was my turn. He was such a sweetheart about it. After the mini golf date was over, he said he was running late for work but "didn't care"; spending time with me was worth being late once.

Our third date was memorable. I suggested we go strawberry picking at a farm near his house; I had grown up going to that farm with my family. He'd never tried that and was open to the idea. I wore jeans, a purple, form-fitting T-shirt, my hair in a ponytail, and a hat. I was meeting him at ten thirty that morning and was running late as usual. My mom said I was "awfully dressed up" to go strawberry picking, and I said I was going with Jack, and she said, "Oh, now I get it!"

I got there about fifteen minutes late and saw him parked across the dusty parking lot but tried to play it cool until he texted me. "Hey, I see your car. I'll come over." We walked to the patch and began picking. I apologized for being late, and he asked how long my ride had taken. When I said I live forty minutes from the farm, he replied, "Oh, man. I feel like a real jerk. I didn't realize it was that far. I will come out to your area from now on."

I kept insisting it wasn't a problem, and we happily filled our baskets as the sweat dripped down my back, and I cursed myself for wearing jeans. I'm pretty sure I had sweat stains on my shirt too, but they didn't seem to bother Jack, because after he paid for our berries, he suggested we go take a look at the animals in their pen.

"Here, let me hold your hand," he said as we walked over, and I almost passed out. I felt myself get even more sweaty and suddenly realized I had no idea how to hold a guy's hand, so I held it in the most awkward way possible, basically crushing his fingers. There was nothing dainty (or intelligent) about the way I held his hand. Then, to make matters even better, the animals decided to have sex in front of us. That wasn't uncomfortable at all for someone on his or her third date. As the one horse humped the other horse and the cows moaned, I wanted to die.

I managed a nervous laugh and said, "I should be going." I asked Jack what he had planned for the rest of the day, and he said he was getting a haircut, and that night was his graduation from community college. I hugged him and wished him well at graduation, and when I got home and told my mom about our date, she said it was impressive that he'd taken the time out to meet me on his graduation day. I thought so too and went out and bought him a fun gift for graduation, so the next time I saw him, I could congratulate him.

The following week we had a movie date at the theater near me. My theater had an event on Tuesdays; I could get two free tickets, so I picked them up in advance and scrambled, trying to find a movie a guy would like. Romantic movies were out; this was only our fourth date, and after seeing the animals having sex, I wasn't ready to sit next to him in a dark room as human beings had sex in front of us on a jumbo screen. I picked some Russell Crowe movie and pulled into the theater (late again), worried he was inside already, waiting for me. But he called me to say he was lost.

He got out of the car at a sleazy Budget Inn to ask the owner for directions, and the owner told him in broken English that he'd passed the theater by quite a bit. Nonetheless, we got inside and got seats, and the movie began. I found it very hard to concentrate and was lost (and bored) throughout most of it. Plus, I constantly worried about whether he was going to try to put his arm around me or grab my hand or, God forbid, even kiss me.

No, it's a crowded theater. Relax. He would have to be an idiot to try a move like that in here. That's what I kept telling myself.

But what would happen afterward? I drove him to his car since he'd shown up so late; he'd ended up basically parking miles away from the theater. As I came to a stop outside his car and kept my car running, we made the usual small talk about the rest of the week. He kept fidgeting and then looked over at me. I sensed what was happening here. He wanted to kiss me. I panicked and felt the sweat start to form on my body.

"Well, have a good night. Text me when you get home!" I practically screamed, and he looked at me and jumped out of the car. My heart was racing, but I just wasn't ready for a kiss, plus I had no idea how.

I dodged that bullet, at least for the time being, but the following Tuesday, we went to see another movie. This time it was a Tom Cruise action flick that was as equally bad and boring, and the theater was half empty. The movie ended around eleven o'clock, and we both stood outside our cars in the parking lot and talked for two hours. A car drove past at one point to head to the nearby McDonald's, and a few guys yelled out the window for us "to get a room!"

As if seeing the animals having sex at the farm wasn't bad enough, this had to happen. I don't think Jack heard, or if he did, he pretended not to. We kept talking and then hugged good-bye. We texted back and forth that weekend (Memorial Day weekend), and the following week was my birthday. He texted me at exactly midnight to wish me a happy birthday and said he'd stayed up because he "wanted to be the first person to wish me a happy birthday." My heart melted. In typical fashion, Sierra was the first person to call me at midnight to wish me a happy birthday, and when I told her Jack had technically beat her to it with the text message, she was (jokingly) upset.

That weekend Sierra and a bunch of my friends took me out to celebrate turning twenty-three, and just as I was finished getting ready, Jack called me. He wanted to wish me a fun night out at the bars (he wouldn't turn twenty-one until later that summer, so he couldn't come out), and then our conversation kept going and going, until I was very late for Sierra's house. The birthday girl was late to her own party.

But that conversation was a turning point because he'd said he couldn't wait for the weather to get warm so he could hit the beach, and I agreed. He asked me what beach I went to, and I said, "Oh, my family has only ever gone to one beach down the shore—Island Beach State Park. It's our favorite." He laughed and said that was the *only* beach he had ever gone to as well. I felt a chill run up my spine. Out of all the beaches at the Jersey Shore, we'd grown up going to the same one? We were soul mates; it was in that moment that I realized I was falling for him.

Jack and I made plans to go bowling the following week after my birthday, and I couldn't wait to see him. He told me he had a gift for me and had something to ask me, but that was a surprise too. I was no dummy. I knew he wasn't asking whether I was a Gemini or Cancer. He was going to ask me to be his girlfriend. The Thursday of our bowling date was sunny and warm; June 10, 2010, was pretty uneventful in the daytime hours, except for when I got a phone call from my friend Sharrie. She had just come back from vacation, and the guy online she was talking to had told her he'd met someone else during the *one week* she was away.

She was crushed, and I felt bad, so I asked whether she wanted to come bowling to get her mind off being dumped. Jack was so easygoing and didn't mind at all; plus Sharrie really liked bowling, so we were all having a good time. I wore jean capris and a blue Hollister T-shirt I had worn a dozen times before; I had my hair all big and curly as usual. I looked cute and casual, which was just the look I was going for to mark one of the biggest nights of my life.

Sharrie and I went to use the bathroom after bowling, and she turned to me. "He likes country music and tennis? If you don't want him, I will take him!" That was her way of saying he was a real catch. Jack emerged from the men's bathroom and asked whether we were interested in going to the diner down the road. Sharrie and I had actually discussed this possibility earlier in the bathroom, with her asking whether it was okay if she came out, should he invite us.

"It's your call—I don't want to ruin your date night," she said. I insisted it was fine.

We sat in a booth at the diner, ordering our meals, and Jack offered to pay the bill for all three of us. Sharrie paid the tip and then mentioned that my car was still sitting in the bowling alley parking lot, since she'd driven me over to the diner and Jack had followed. He quickly piped up that he would be glad to drive me back to my car. My heart raced, and I felt myself starting to perspire as Sharrie told us to have fun and winked at me.

It was our first time alone together in his car, and the drive to the bowling alley was quick. He handed me my birthday gift, which was wrapped so neatly that I was sad to open it. He gave me a DVD series for a popular show, one we had joked a lot about. The gift was sweet because it showed he'd listened.

We arrived at my car, yet we sat in his car and talked and talked. Just as I saw the clock flicker to midnight, I reached for the handle and thanked him for the gift and for taking me bowling. "Hey, wait one second. I want to ask you something," he said, just barely above a whisper.

My heart raced, and I felt my mouth turn dry. "Sure thing," I said in the most casual tone I could.

"I really like spending time with you and think you are a great girl. I was wondering if you would be my girlfriend," he said, and I felt a huge smile forming on my face.

"Yes, I would like that a lot," I said.

"Cool—that's great!"

He looked at me for a kiss, but I was still too nervous, so I kept blabbering on and on about something, and he said, "There is something you should know. I have a disease called ulcerative colitis." He explained that he'd been a healthy kid, always playing baseball and going out with friends, but when he turned sixteen, he started to feel sick; and after going to various doctors for many tests, it came back that he had this gastrointestinal disease. I asked whether he was terminally ill (I was really scared), and he laughed and said no, but he did take eleven pills a day and didn't eat or drink very much.

We talked in his car for a long time about his disease until I realized it was now one o'clock in the morning, and the employees had all gone home. Just our two cars were sitting in this bowling alley on the side of a highway. Despite his forty-minute ride home, he announced he was putting our relationship on Facebook the minute he got home, and I insisted I was going to bed and would "accept" it in the morning. The following morning when I did, my phone began ringing off the hook, and tons of friends were writing on my Facebook wall to give us their congratulations. I felt on top of the world. Our official anniversary was June 11, 2010, a date forever etched in my mind.

The summer was in full swing, and immediately I was eager to have dates with Jack and show him off to all my friends and family. My first real boyfriend! At age twenty-three. Better late than never. All while I'd carefully avoided kissing him. The thought made me sick to my stomach. I was twenty-three, had never kissed a boy, and had no idea how. Where do you put your hands? Who closes their eyes first? Who leans? What if you have stinky breath? Ugh, it was all a mess, and I thought the longer I could avoid that, the better, since I was going to make a fool out of myself anyway.

One night I was lying in bed when he texted and asked whether he could ask me a question. Uh-oh. I said yes, and he asked, "When are we going to have a first kiss?"

I was mortified. "I am not sure—I have not done that before and don't know how."

He replied that he didn't know how either, but "how about we both try it together?" And I smiled and agreed.

Later that month my family was going to London to visit my cousins and see the sights. We loved London and had gone once when I was fourteen, and I had gone there during my senior year in college for a week for a class. I told Jack I would miss him and would see him when I got home. I was babysitting one afternoon before the trip, suddenly felt bold, and asked whether he wanted to come to my house for dinner the night before we left for the UK.

Dinner was great, and when I walked him out to his car, I asked whether he could purchase tickets for the newest Twilight movie coming out. Opening day was right when I got home, and I knew tickets would be sold out. He said he would grab the tickets and take me right after I got home. Our family trip to Europe was nothing short of amazing; we took in all the sights and also visited our family in the countryside. A day trip to Paris also proved to be amusing; I remember posing atop the Eiffel Tower and just knew this summer was going to be special.

I had jet lag, so I slept in the next day after we arrived home and awoke only when the doorbell rang in the early afternoon. "Who the heck could that be?" my mom wondered aloud. It was a floral delivery for me. Jack had sent me a beautiful bouquet of summer flowers with a note saying he hoped my trip was good and that he couldn't wait to see me that night for the movie.

We had a great time at the movies that night, and we sat talking in his car afterward, since he'd picked me up and driven me there. I gave him the souvenir I'd purchased for him, and he looked right at me, wanting a kiss, but I was still scared. I looked away, and he drove us back to his house. We talked the entire way. *Whew.*

Well, he pulled up outside my darkened house, and the conversation grew quiet. "How about a good-night kiss?" he suggested. I glanced over at my house and saw it was dark; everyone appeared to be sleeping, not watching us with binoculars.

"Umm, how about a kiss on the cheek?" I suggested, and he did so. Then, not knowing what to do, I gave him one too. I hopped out of his car and was mortified for turning him down due to being anxious.

A week later he came by to pick me up for dinner at a local place in town, and I wore a cute sundress and had asked my neighbor do my hair and makeup. I came down the stairs with her, and the sun was gleaming through our foyer, and I had to squint when I said hello to him. He met my friend next door, and she texted me as she was walking home that he was the best guy for me.

We had a nice time at dinner and had a great conversation about London and the PR/marketing internship I was going to be starting the week afterward at the nearby hospital system. We got back to my house and were outside his car, talking, when suddenly he leaned in and took charge. We kissed.

Nothing went wrong. It all went quite smooth actually. For two people who had no idea what they were doing, it went quite well. I was relieved. But as the days went on and the summer got hotter, I was nervous for a second and third kiss. I was worried that my face would be all red or my makeup would be all sticky as he leaned in for a kiss. I worried that he would smell my perspiration from the warmth of the sun. So for the next few dates, kisses weren't part of them. We kissed once, but not every date revolved around doing that.

As time went on, we kissed more but only when parting. It was a quick kiss good-bye, not a make-out session. I had no idea how to do that either and was in no place to suggest figuring it out. A good-night kiss was nerve wracking enough.

Jack met me at my internship every week for lunch, even though on many of those days, he never ate or drank anything. Some days he ordered a grilled cheese sandwich and French fries, and he smiled at my boss as she said hello to us in the line to pay. I only had an hour for lunch and his ride to my office was thirty-five minutes, but he never complained. We had the best times during those lunches.

July rolled around, and there was an Amish fair near Kutztown University, and I thought it would be a fun day trip for Jack and me, so I posted it on his Facebook, asking, "What do you think?" Well, he never acknowledged the post, and I asked him again through text, but he sort of brushed it off. So I asked Jo Jo and Lin to go, and we decided to leave early the following morning to make the two-hour trip to Pennsylvania for this Amish fair.

I was in bed, and Jack texted me that he wanted to tell me something. "Go ahead," I prompted, ready to hear something I wasn't going to like.

"I love you," he said. I was floored. We had been dating only one month and had met only three months before.

"I wish you would have said it the first time in person," I said, to which he said he was going to call me right then and there and say it aloud. I giggled in my bed and said he couldn't because my door was open and my family was asleep, and I didn't want to wake anyone. It would have to wait for when we saw each other next.

The fair turned out to a bust; it was extremely hot, and there wasn't much to see or buy. I later found out Jack hated long car rides, because he was anxious about being without a bathroom for such a long period of time. I wished I hadn't pushed so much and gotten mad over his not responding to the Amish fair, but think it worked out for the best. *Plus, he loved me!*

I met Jack's family in early August. He carefully wrote down directions, going backstreets to avoid rush hour traffic; and as I pulled up, I glanced around and took it all in. His house was modest but pleasant looking. He took me through the garage, and I immediately met his mother, who was at the stove stirring a pot. We made our way into the living room, where I met his father and older brother. We ate in the dining room, and I was so hungry but didn't want to overdo it or talk with food in my mouth, so I ate slowly and quietly. We all talked throughout dinner, and the conversation lingered afterward as well.

Jack was starting at his new university in two weeks and needed to circle activities he wanted to take part in at orientation the following week. "You circled everything but lunch!" I joked, to which his dad roared with laughter. I was just teasing, but Jack rarely took part in activities that involved food due to his stomach disease. We all shared some of the banana cream pie I'd whipped up for dessert, and I thanked his family for dinner and told his mother I loved her homemade salad dressing.

Jack asked whether I wanted to go for a drive to see where he'd grown up, and he grabbed his keys. He took me to his middle school (where I'd played tennis in high school), then to his high school, and so forth. Each time we pulled into a dark parking lot, all I could think of was, *He is doing this purposely to make out with me. I know how this stuff works. They call it parking!* My heart raced, but I was quite wrong. Jack had no ulterior motives; he truly wanted to show me where he'd grown up.

When we got back to his darkened house, everyone was fast asleep. We watched TV, and then I drove home. I liked how friendly and loving his family was. His dad told Jack that I was "a keeper" and told him to make sure I didn't get away. He said it was evident by my friendly demeanor and impeccable manners that I had been "clearly raised right."

Jack invited me over for dinner once a week, and he also came to my house once a week. I picked up pretty quickly on how much his family enjoyed staying home—on their sofa. His parents never seemed to go anywhere alone, and family time was every day, it seemed. They were so happy to see me each time I came over, and Jack lit up like a child at Christmas each time he saw how well I got along with his family.

Yet I was always a bit perplexed about how hard it was for us have alone time. They had one TV in the living room, and that was the main room in the house. And immediately following dinner, everyone ran into the room and watched whatever was on TV that evening. At my house, we had multiple rooms with TVs, and people had multiple activities going on. My mom went out with friends, my brother was out with his friends, and my sister often had friends over to dye their hair in our bathroom sink or paint nails in the basement. There was always something going on in our house, and it had always been like that.

Jack's family was wonderful but very different from mine. His mom worked full-time but spent hours each day cooking dinner for "her men." Dinner often included a soup or salad, a loaf of bread, and a main course consisting of meat, rice, and two sides of vegetables. Yet there were times when Jack was out with me and missed dinner, and his mother would get upset. One of these episodes occurred when we spent the afternoon picking peaches at a nearby farm and then went to my cousin's house-warming party. We started off at the farm in the late afternoon and kept sitting down to take breaks due to how hot it was. After we picked a ton of peaches and rode the hayride back, he called his mom to say we may be late for dinner. I couldn't hear her response, but I knew it wasn't a positive one, due to his facial expression. She was clearly upset we were going to be late to dinner, and Jack was now stressed over it.

We got to the crowded party and there were about fifty people crammed around, with only three faces I recognized. Jack went to the upstairs bathroom as I ate and tried to mingle, but no one seemed that interested in talking to me. We stayed for about an hour and then realized how uncomfortable we both felt in such a large setting where we hardly knew anyone. We made the twenty-five-minute ride to his house. There we found his dad on the couch with the brother (Mom had already gone to bed), and his dad warmed up our hamburgers and hot dogs, and chatted with us. It was close to nine o'clock, and we were starving.

During our trips to Island Beach, Jack wouldn't consume a morsel yet still managed to go to the bathroom once or twice. His body was so sick that anything he consumed went right through him. I never realized how sick he was, because he hardly told me. At most he moaned and said, "My stomach hurts." He excused himself and headed to the bathroom multiple times throughout our date. I tried my best to take care of him by preparing neutral foods for snacks and encouraging him to try the healthy treats I'd baked.

I was left in the dark and never knew how severe his disease could get until the day I looked up more information online and saw that people with that disease can get colon cancer due to their colons being so severely damaged. I was worried that he would die one day and leave me all alone, like my dad had done to my mom. I felt sick, and that's when I realized just how sick and serious Jack's disease was, and I felt sorry for him at the same time. I was sorry he'd woken one day sick, sorry he wasn't able to take part in the activities most guys his age were doing, and sorry he was so nervous all the time that at any given moment he could have an accident if a bathroom wasn't nearby.

However, I really introduced Jack to life. By dating me, he was opened up to a world of fun. Our three-month anniversary fell in early September, and I thought it would be fun to head into the city to see a Broadway show and have a nice dinner. These were things my parents and friends always did, so why not? I had no idea Jack never went into the city.

I was so eager to make the most of our first trip into New York City together that I got up extra early that day and got a haircut and blowout with the same girl who'd done my hair for our first date. I picked out a fun outfit and was beaming when Jack showed up in the Ralph Lauren polo I had given him for our one-month anniversary. Off we went to walk Central Park before heading to see *Rock of Ages*. Then we had dinner at an Italian restaurant in the Village. We got off the bus and made our way into the heart of Times Square, and suddenly Jack stopped and looked up at "all the tall buildings."

"Get out of the way!" people muttered under their breaths while I grabbed his arm.

I said, "What are you doing? You can't just stop in the middle of a New York City walkway!" Then I specifically asked him how many times he had been to the city.

"Really, never," he said, and I was speechless. I'd come in every year as a kid for the Macy's Thanksgiving Day Parade and then again around Christmas to see the tree and *The Radio City Christmas Spectacular*. While my friends were out getting sloshed down the shore for prom weekend, my family took me to Madame Tussauds Wax Museum, then dinner at my favorite Italian restaurant, which was how I wanted to spend my eighteenth birthday weekend. I always went into the city and knew my way around. I was shocked his parents had never taken him and that he had no idea where he was the whole day, but I enjoyed playing tour guide.

The day turned out to be one of the more gorgeous days in September. We approached the Central Park subway station, and he asked me how much a ticket was. Then he proceeded to pull out his stuffed wallet and loudly say, "I don't think I have two singles … I only have fifties."

"Do you want to get mugged? Put that away!" I yelled, and we hopped onto a subway heading downtown, which would be the same direction Jack was about to fall. The subway was full, and he didn't know to grab onto the railing as it moved, so he almost fell backward. I grabbed him and told him to always hold on. I didn't know it was his first time on the subway.

Alas, we made it down to the Village without Jack getting us killed or mugged. The eatery was small and intimate; a candlelight dinner of bread and gnocchi awaited us. The food was delicious, and we had such an incredible day and night. He kept saying how much he enjoyed our day and wanted to go back again.

October rolled around, and I signed us up for a candlelight walk for leukemia one Saturday night. I signed us up in memory of Poppy, and we were eager to walk for a good cause and then order a pizza with my sister back at home later. The night was a little chiller than we thought, so Jack gave me his hoodie to wear. I liked smelling like him and was happy to wear it. Earlier in the week, we were watching a movie at each of our homes and texting throughout it. During one of the make-out scenes, Jack texted me, "I want to kiss like that." And I once again replied, "It looks nice, but I have no idea how to do that." He suggested we try it over the weekend.

And so we did. We got back from the walk and ate pizza with Lin, while the whole time I was silently wishing she would stay the entire night, and he was silently wishing she would eat her pizza little faster. When she did leave, Jack got up to head to the bathroom, and I put in the movie we had both decided to watch, *Dirty Dancing*. Jack had never seen it, and I thought it would be fun for our first make-out session.

Who the heck plans their first make-out session? We did—down to the time, movie, and couch. He sauntered back in from the bathroom, and I felt myself get nervous all of a sudden. We sat and watched Patrick Swayze gyrate across the screen until Jack started to play with my ponytail, then massage my shoulders, and then ... Well, you catch my drift. Making out wasn't as difficult as we both had thought.

Then Christmas rolled around, and Santa came to town. Literally. Jack went all out for holidays, and Christmas was no exception. While I planned the perfect trip into New York City (complete with seeing the tree, going to another Broadway show, and getting cupcakes at Magnolia Bakery), Jack was busy planning the perfect gifts for me. He went to the local butcher in his area, brought my family gourmet meats and ate dinner with us the night my mom cooked them. Then he and I exchanged gifts little by little. We had an "Eight Days of Christmas," as my mom referred to it as, and rolled her eyes as his gifts kept coming in.

While there were so many happy times with Jack, there were also times when I felt confused and left out in the dark. For example, on one Friday night, he took me out to a nice restaurant nearby we liked. I had just worked a full day at my full-time magazine job and then rushed home to shower and change and told him to come at seven thirty. When the doorbell rang at 7:10, I lost it.

"Who the hell could that be? It better not be him, because I told him seven thirty!" I bellowed, not realizing my voice echoed throughout our castle-like house.

My mom yelled right back at me. "What would you like me to do? Hurry up and dry your hair and change!" She let him in; then she slipped a note under the bathroom door for me, which read, "HE'S HERE." I rushed downstairs and would have loved to have put on more makeup and make my hair look nicer, but he was so early.

We got to the restaurant, and Jack was withdrawn and wouldn't look at me or talk to me too much. I wondered why I was there. I tried asking him about his current mood, but he brushed it off and then excused himself to use the men's room. I sat at the table and stared into space, wishing he would tell me what was wrong, but he never did. He later said his disease was bothering him, and he typically experienced flare-ups and discomfort, and he had trouble focusing on anything positive.

A few months later was my twenty-fourth birthday, and I was so excited for my first birthday with a boyfriend, and then a week later was our one-year anniversary. That weekend my family was having our annual birthday barbecue for me, Aunt Jo, and Marisa. Jack was set to come and see everyone when he announced that morning that he wouldn't be attending. He called me, saying he was "coming down with something" and didn't want to get my cousins sick.

It was early June, the party was outside in the fresh air, and he had the sniffles. I was so upset and tried to shrug it off, but one of my cousins approached me inside my kitchen during the party and asked why he wasn't there and wondered whether everything was all right between us. My eyes watered, and I said, "Yes, he's just not feeling well."

"Oh, it's okay. Are you two fighting?" she asked.

And I said no, not at all; he was just sick. But in the back of my mind, I wondered how sick he was. I didn't think the beginning of a sore throat was enough to miss your girlfriend's birthday after the first year of dating her. I often went to school and work sick, unless I was really feeling ill; then I stayed home. Instead of expressing my feelings to Jack, I acted immaturely and ignored him. *For two whole days.*

It wasn't until that Tuesday evening that my friend Derrick (who occasionally texted back and forth with Jack) told me Jack was really worried about me and wondered where I was.

I came back with, "Like he really gives a hoot!"

When Jack called me again that night, I broke down and answered, and he really let me have it. "You are so selfish; let's call a spade a spade, Katrina. You didn't give a shit that I was sick and probably never gave shit about me in the first place. All you cared about was me coming to your little birthday party."

I cried on the phone and told him I did care, but his cold was minor, and my extended family hardly saw him because he never came to our functions. He made a comment that maybe this was a sign we weren't meant to be, but I convinced him to give me another chance.

As I sat there on my closet floor, the thought of losing Jack was right there on the table, but I couldn't let that happen. I talked about losing my dad and cousin, and said that I couldn't imagine losing him too. I convinced him so much to stay with me that the two-hour conversation ended with him saying, "I love you so much. You know that, right? I'm sorry for all of this. Let's put this behind us." I breathed a sigh of relief.

Our first anniversary was the following week, and he came over that rainy Saturday afternoon, and we exchanged gifts in my kitchen. He gave me a beautiful Fossil watch with our names and anniversary date engraved in it, tied to the wrist of a tie-dyed Build-A-Bear he'd made for me. I got him a gift cardholder and had fun picking out gift cards to all his favorite places and attaching them to this. He suggested we walk around Hoboken and try the famed Carlo's Bakery, and my eyes lit up.

We had such a nice anniversary walking around Hoboken and taking in the New York skyline. We split a deli sandwich and picked up a cake from the bakery before heading back to our favorite eatery near my house. This time he was totally focused on me, and we had a really good time. He wore a plaid Ralph Lauren blue button-down shirt I had bought him, and he looked hot. A man in plaid will always get a second glance from me. After dinner and cake, we talked for hours. He left around three o'clock in the morning and texted me when he got home, as always. Things were going great, and I was so happy.

We spent the rest of the summer at the shore, and for Labor Day weekend we drove up to Mystic, Connecticut, for the day. It was a long day trip, with some traffic and tons of activity. His dad had advised him not to go due to his stomach and how tired he would get, but he was a trooper. (His family, however, spent the entire long weekend on their sofa, getting up only when it was time for grilling hot dogs and hamburgers.) I saw how nervous he was that morning before we embarked on our trip. He paced around my kitchen and wouldn't eat a morsel.

"It's a two-and-a-half-hour ride—are you sure you don't want any food?" I asked.

But he said no. He went to the bathroom about three times until finally I said we needed to get on the road. We took turns driving, and he took me to the Mohegan Sun Casino, where I won $150 and turned right around and bought my very own Michael Kors purse at the outlets for $150. We took a sunset boat ride and ate at Mystic Pizza. We were exhausted, but it was time to head back.

Then before we knew it, fall was upon us. Jack headed into his senior year of college, and I worked forty hours a week at a magazine job I hated.

Jack sent flowers to the office one especially difficult day, with a note telling me to try to enjoy my day. My boss, who had the personality of a wet mop, walked past, forced a grin, and said, "Anniversary?" as she gestured to the beautiful bouquet.

I nodded, suddenly embarrassed to say, "No, they are just because he felt like it." I was never a girl boys liked, so I was still trying to wrap my brain around the fact that he'd sent them to me for no real occasion, except for the fact that my job sucked.

We celebrated the holidays separately, since his family typically ended up going down the shore to see his grandma, aunt, and cousins, while our gatherings were close by. As the holiday season approached, our beloved dog, Lucky, started getting sick. He wasn't eating much, and all he wanted to do was lie around. Seeing this decline killed us, but we held out hope that maybe he was just under the weather. Jack always played with him, and so did everyone else who came over; he was truly the most beautiful golden retriever anyone had seen.

My mom had booked a trip a few months before with some friends to go to Mexico in December. It was her first big trip since my dad passed away, and she was eager for some fun in the sun. While she was gone, Lucky took a turn for the worst. I was on my hands and knees, trying to feed him dog food, but he refused to even look at it. I tried giving him pretzels and animal crackers, and that did the trick for a little while, but then he wouldn't drink or move much.

Every December Jack's family went to Brooklyn to see his aunt and "The Lights," which consisted of houses decorated to the extreme for the holiday season. Those living in the homes go above and beyond, spending thousands of dollars on their electric bill to pay for these lights. They were going that Saturday night, and I was invited and so excited. I loved being included in their family activities and was eager to see what all the fuss was about. However, when I saw how sick my pooch was, I knew there was no way I could leave him. With my mom gone, I was running the show, and I was heartbroken just to picture leaving him alone in the house for the entire evening.

I told Jack I couldn't go, and he did something that shocked me. He told his family to go ahead without him, and he came to my house and spent the night in sweatpants with me, trying to feed Lucky pretzels.

We received word a few days later that Lucky had cancer and didn't have much time. Christmas was approaching, and my mom was away; and on top of this, suddenly the house was freezing. It turned out that the furnace was broken. We were supposed to call her in Mexico only for emergencies, but between these two events, we called a lot more. She was going to come back early, but my siblings and I told her there was no need to; we would handle things.

My uncle brought over space heaters, and that kept us somewhat warm at night. And we were at work and school in the daytime, so then it was fine. The next two weeks were hard, and we watched Lucky have trouble walking around, and his eyes looked so sad as he sat on the floor. I was mad at myself for going out so much over the years and not spending enough time with him. Jack told me it wasn't fair to blame myself, but I did.

Lucky collapsed in our house on Christmas day, right before my entire family was due to arrive. My brother's girlfriend started crying, and my mom left food cooking in the kitchen to come and see what was happening, and we all lost it. As if my family hadn't already experienced enough grief, now my dog was dropping dead on our floor on Christmas Day.

I called Jack and cried my eyes out as I told him what Lucky looked like and what was happening. That Christmas Jack's family decided they had seen the family enough on Christmas Eve and were just going to celebrate with the four of them at their house. *On that same beloved sofa.* Jack never offered to come to our house (not even for dessert) and didn't say anything on the phone after I told him my dog was downstairs dying.

At the time, I didn't beg him to come. I didn't think I needed to. I wanted him there as I cried, but he never offered, and I didn't push.

Winter rolled on, and it was our second Valentine's Day before I knew it. We celebrated that Saturday, which was Lin's birthday, but she had plans with friends that night, so I didn't feel bad going out with Jack. We were due to receive snow that day, so in the days prior, he changed his plans for our big date night. I had told him during the month before to surprise me, since I'd planned our entire Valentine's Day outing the year before. His brother suggested dinner and a movie since we didn't often do an outing as simple as that. We went to a nice Italian place and then went to see *The Vow.* Snow fell a bit that morning but was fine by the time night rolled around. As we sat in the restaurant, I started getting text messages from my friends, stating that Whitney Houston had died. I checked online, and sure enough, the rumors were true.

The week after that, I was off to Las Vegas with Jo Jo. It was our first time out there and our first trip together, and we were ecstatic. Jack was sad to see me go but told me he was happy when I took little trips like that because it gave him a chance to "relax and just breathe." My life often resembles the Energizer Bunny, and I was always making plans for him and me, so my being away for a few days was a nice break for him. Jack lives far from the airport and wasn't well traveled, but I flew once a year, so I thought he would offer to take me to the airport or pick me up.

Nope. My brother dropped us off, and we paid forty-five dollars for a car service to bring us back to my cousin's house the night we returned. Jack came to her condo complex, though, to bring me back to my house. I asked him why he hadn't offered to go to the airport, and his response was, "Just because I am your boyfriend, why does that make me your taxicab?"

I came back with, "It would have been a nice gesture, considering we paid some dude forty-five dollars to bring us home." He then made a quip about how far the airport was and about how he'd flown only once in his entire life, so therefore he knew nothing about the ins and outs of the airport. If he had picked us up, maybe we should have just paid *him* the forty-five dollars then. When he said it like that, I actually thought he was right, and I was the crazy one for even suggesting he pick us up in the first place.

My twenty-fifth birthday was on the horizon, and so was Jack's graduation. Jack and his family go to Atlantic City about ten times a year. They eat, sleep, and breathe the casinos and nice restaurants. They go so often that they receive numerous rewards such as free rooms or parking. He and his brother mentioned the idea of going down for my twenty-fifth birthday that June, and I was on board. They booked a huge suite right after I got home from Vegas. With his brother's rewards, the room came out to be a great price, and I in turn invited about thirteen friends to come and stay, and each chipped in.

I was so excited for June to arrive, but first we were in full graduation mode. Jack was set to earn his diploma in early May, and as the days inched closer to it, he started to get cold feet. He didn't want a party, dinner, or gifts; and now he was nervous about walking in the ceremony due to the lack of a bathroom. I tried telling him he'd worked incredibly hard for this day and owed it to himself to walk or even just attend it, but he leaned toward not going at all. His family did nothing to sway his opinion, but I'm a fighter, and I kept pushing him. I told him he had walked in his community college graduation two years before, right when we'd begun dating. I didn't attend that ceremony, because we'd just met, but he'd told me he went.

I got two subs for my five-hour shift at the YMCA and had bought an orange sundress the month before. I spent the previous night baking a cake for him and wrapping the gifts I had worked so hard to find. Then I received a text from him bright and early that Saturday morning. "Hey, Katrina. I will not be attending graduation today."

My heart dropped. I called him, and he was very curt and said it was his decision, and he didn't think it was a good idea. I was done arguing with him over this, and his family just dropped the subject altogether. I cried and paced back and forth in my kitchen. I was already up, so I went to the eight o'clock boot camp class at the gym and was half asleep as I jumped through tires and lifted dumbbells. I cried in the shower and mourned the beautiful day in his life he was missing out on: taking pictures with family and friends, shaking hands with teachers at his small college where everyone knew one another. His missing out was too much to bear.

My mom told me to just drive over to his house with the gifts and cake. "He is hurting over this decision more that you know and more than he will ever tell you. Just go there and support him." I hopped in the car and drove there, and his father looked surprised when he came to the door.

Jack said, "Hey there—what are you doing here?" After dating for almost two years now, I needed a reason to show up? I gave him the cake and stuttered that I wanted to see him. Everyone was just hanging around at noon on a gorgeous day, not addressing the elephant in the room. His mother picked up food to grill, and his dad invited me to stay. "Yeah, you can stay," Jack muttered as he paced the living room.

I suddenly felt sick and out of place. My heart raced, and I suddenly felt sweaty. I didn't know what to do. I felt more awkward than I'd envisioned during my ride there, and I really wanted to just talk to him alone and hug him. That was never an option in our relationship unless he came to my house; his family was always home and *right there.*

The happy moments I'd envisioned were gone. I suddenly needed to get out of there. He walked me out to my car, and I hugged and kissed him good-bye, and I cried the minute I pulled out onto the main road. I could barely see due to my tears. I was angry, and my stomach was in knots. I had a book with me and drove to a nearby lake I had never had been to; I sat on a picnic table alone. As I left Jack, I told him I was going there to lay out and read. He either didn't get my hint to come along or pretended not to.

All afternoon as I sat, cried, and read, I looked anxiously at the parking lot, waiting for his silver car to pull in. When the exact make and model he had pulled in, my heart dropped. He had really come! Then I saw a fifty-year-old black man climb out of the car. Sigh.

He didn't text me, and I called Rachel and Angelica. I cried my eyes out in the park, explaining how the day had played out. Angelica later said the phone call had made her so sad because what was supposed to be a beautiful day had ended up being awkward and lonely. Rachel, on the other hand, could smell the angle I was coming from and asked how I felt about the relationship altogether.

I blurted out that I wasn't so sure anymore. I was tired of pushing Jack to do things when his family didn't. I was starting to get depressed from his glum outlook on life and the way he let his disease control him. I wanted the happy Jack back from the summer of 2010. Right after I hung up from Rachel and the sun began to set, I packed up my book, and Jack texted me.

"How's the park?" Then he came back with, "Everything OK?"

I wept as I read his texts and had to be honest with him. I said I needed some time to think things over and couldn't see him for a week or two. I thought time would heal things. Then it was Memorial Day weekend two weeks later, and despite some texting with him here and there, we didn't see each other. Derrick slept over at my house for the weekend while my mom went away and thought it would be fun if we drove up to Pennsylvania and went outlet shopping and then toured Bushkill Falls ("The Niagara of the West"), so we lathered up with sunscreen and set out on this scorching hot day. I asked Derrick whether we could make a pit stop at Jack's on the way home, since we were passing his exit anyway and had packed his graduation gift. I even went as far as to wrap his gift in blue diploma wrapping paper. I thought maybe an impromptu visit would ease the pain of the past two weeks.

We toured the falls and took some beautiful pictures before stopping by the outlets and then arriving at Jack's house close to dinnertime. He texted me throughout the day to ask how the ride up was and how the falls looked, but he had no idea we were coming over. His family had no plans the entire weekend, so he was home, and I knew how Jack operated. He didn't like surprises, and since my "spontaneous" visit on his graduation day hadn't gone so well, the last thing I wanted was to piss him off more.

I casually texted him when we were close to his exit and asked him to meet us outside, and he did. I could barely look him in the eye after how awkward our last encounter had been, so I looked at the ground while Derrick rambled on about how gorgeous the rushing water had looked at the falls. I could feel Jack looking at me, studying my face to see what I was thinking. I finally looked at him and said, "Well, I have a little something for you—you know, for graduation and all." I reached into the backseat for his gift.

"Oh no, you didn't. I am so stupid—I don't deserve this," he said. "God, I am such an idiot. Thank you very much for this." I instructed him to go ahead and open it, and when he did, his lips formed into a smile, and he grinned from ear to ear.

"Do you like it?" I shyly asking, suddenly feeling like I had just met him, not that he was my boyfriend of two years. He said he did and motioned toward the house, saying that it was time for dinner, and he had to go. But he loved the gift.

Then it was birthday time! I was excited to go to Atlantic City with my friends and Jack's friends to ring in the big event. As always, Jack was stressed and nervous. We arrived at the hotel, and all four of us girls headed to the lobby to meet him and his brother. We got there early that Friday afternoon to kick-start the weekend. Of course, the security guard stopped us and asked to see our room key.

"We're with them." We gestured to Jack and his brother, but the guard was quick to warn us about the limit of people allowed per room. He walked away, and we were confused because Jack had rented a huge suite, and there were only six of us right now; his other best friend was in the room, and I had more people coming later. The guard stood by the escalator, and Jack took this as meaning he wouldn't let us up.

"C'mon, just walk past him!" I instructed everyone. When no one moved, I grabbed my purse and suitcase and led the way.

"Jesus Christ, here we go," Jack mumbled and was so nervous we were going to get caught.

"Jack, people rent these rooms and squeeze fifty people into them for parties; we have six people here. Let's go," I said, rolling my eyes behind his back.

We made our way up the escalator and met up with another friend of mine who had arrived, and we all proceeded up the elevator to our suite with an ocean view. I straightened my hair and wore this sparkly tank top and leggings ensemble I had purchased the week before. We all had so much fun at dinner, and then we walked the boardwalk and went to the casinos.

While I was sharing a story with the gals, Jack apparently said to Angelica, "I am so excited to see what outfit Katrina wears tomorrow night!" I blushed when she repeated this to me.

Saturday morning arrived, and the sun was gleaming. It truly was a gorgeous day, and I was excited to lay out. But when I woke up, Jack was nowhere to be found, and I was a little bummed. His brother was gone too, and their friend told me they had gotten up early to walk the boardwalk. When they strolled back in with orange juice for all of us, I asked why he hadn't awoken me to join him.

"Well, you were with your friends. I didn't want to disturb you," he said, but I wished he had. That would have been a great way to start the day, but now it was bagel time, and I was starving. I'd stopped and gotten bagels and cream cheese the day before, and I'd picked out a poppy bagel just for Jack. Well, he hadn't wanted the bagel and had waved me off when I told him it was for him. In a room full of six people, he basically said he didn't want it, and I felt hurt.

We went to the beach, and I asked Jack where the umbrella was that I had packed in his car. "You know my thoughts on skin cancer," I reminded him, and he realized the umbrella was still in his car.

I offered to go with him to the parking garage, but he said, "No, you're already in your bathing suit with all your friends. I can just go." Off he went, and he was gone almost forty-five minutes. I kept asking his brother and friend where he was and wondered if maybe someone should go check on him; after all, parking garages in general are seedy, and murders have occurred in the ones in Atlantic City.

"I am sure he is fine!" They both shrugged me off and flirted with two of my friends in the water. I swam a bit and then saw Jack walking toward us with no umbrella in hand.

"Hey! Why the fuck didn't you answer your phone?" Jack yelled to his brother. "I tried calling you because I went up and down a few floors and cannot find the car anywhere." His brother reminded him that they'd moved it after going to the liquor store to buy more booze yesterday. Didn't he remember?

"Son of a bitch!" Jack grumbled. Then he turned to me and explained that I would just have to make do without my umbrella.

I got dolled up in a sexy dress that night as more friends arrived for the bash. We ate dinner at this incredible Italian restaurant, and my friends had the waiters sing to me. I enjoyed chocolate cake while we all took pictures at the table. The game plan was to hit up a club afterward, but

Angelica and the boys expressed no desire, so they were going to gamble, but dinner ended close to ten thirty, and I was frankly pooped already.

We nixed the club and just gambled and played more drinking games in the room. I was surprised Jack didn't bust out a cake for me, because there was this fantastic bakery he always preached about down in Atlantic City in a seedy area (what part of Atlantic City isn't seedy?), but it had some decedent goodies. I thought for sure he would have picked up a cake from there, but the night came and went, and there was nothing.

The next morning, as we packed up our belongings to check out of the hotel, I realized all the boys were gone. "Another early-morning stroll on the boardwalk without me?" I muttered to myself. When his friend strolled into the room, he said he had gone gambling, but Jack and his brother had run to do an errand.

In walked Jack with a sheet cake, for Christ's sake, from that bakery. Mind you, it was eleven o'clock in the morning, and we had to leave the room for a noon checkout, and Jack was already freaking out that we were going to be late and that they were going to charge us for another night.

"What about my cake?" I said as we just looked at it in his arms.

"Umm, I'm not sure what you want to do with it. Take it home?" he said. It was already 90 degrees out, and the last thing I wanted to do was put this huge cake into the trunk of my friend's car and let it get smashed. Plus it would have been bad to let it sit out all day, and we were going out to lunch, then to the outlets afterward. Jack clearly hadn't thought this through, and I was disappointed. It would have been much more practical for him to pick up the cake the night before (or even the first night we'd arrived); that way everyone could have enjoyed it and sung to me.

So we ended up leaving the beautiful cake behind with a note for the maids to enjoy it. I was so sad leaving it there, but Jack kept saying it was okay, even when I knew he must have blown about fifty dollars on that cake. He slipped the maid twenty dollars on the way out, and all ten of us made our way down the elevator. My fabulous birthday was over, and summer was just beginning.

Jack had a lot on his mind that June, and I wasn't aware of most of it until we went out to dinner later that month. We had plans to play mini golf and try this new restaurant midway between our houses, and Jack was awfully quiet most of the night. The restaurant was packed, so immediately he felt out of place when we got there.

"They have bathrooms, right?" he asked.

I replied, "It's a restaurant; of course they do." It was a common question he asked me each time we went somewhere new, and we sat in silence, waiting for our number to be called. He looked on edge, but I assumed this was because of how crowded the place was. The food was great, and we were sitting in my car and talking afterwards, when he suddenly said it.

"I have decided to have surgery this summer to get rid of my disease completely. It will be a lengthy operation, and the recovery will be even longer and more intense. I may not be around for a while, so I wanted to see what you wanted to do." His voice trailed off, and he avoided eye contact.

Tears welled up in my eyes. He continued with, "Maybe we should take a break, and you can go on with your life. I'm not going to be a lot of fun for a while. In fact, I will probably be sleeping and shitting all the time as my body adjusts."

I started to sob and begged him to think this over. I asked whether he was certain about the operation and worried about the risks of this six-hour procedure. I insisted that I didn't want to break up and that I wanted to be with him.

The following weekend was Lin and Mikey's double graduation party, and Jack was absent. He was down the shore, visiting his ninety-year-old Grammy (who'd said I was "so beautiful" the summer before when she met me). Then his family took him out to an upscale restaurant on a boat to "celebrate" his making the decision to gain ahold of his life again.

Family members and friends we didn't see too often asked where he was, since they were dying to meet the man who had "finally" become my boyfriend. My great-aunt had heard about Jack and his disease from my mother during phone conversations, and she pulled me aside to chat. "Your mother said he had shingles this past Easter—that is quite serious."

I told her about how I wasn't able to see him for two weeks due to Lin never having the chicken pox and my mom was afraid she would then get it. His parents thought it was wise too, so we talked on the phone, and I dropped off a care package when I was in the area one day, interviewing someone for an article for the newspaper.

My mom made a comment to me one day in the kitchen while Jack was all shingled up, saying, "You know, he is a very sick boy. Shingles is very serious." I told her I was aware of that. I think she was implying that I should think about this relationship, because his illness was already a huge factor, and here he was, getting sicker.

At the graduation party, my great-aunt told me a story about one of her nieces, who was dating a man with lupus. "That man is very sick, and her life would be very hard if she married him." I thought about what she was implying as well. Two family members had told me to really think about Jack and see whether I could handle a life with his illnesses, and I was once again unsure what to think.

My mom's best friend mentioned her niece who had the same disease as Jack. When she and her husband had gone down the shore, they were sometimes stopping ten times along the Parkway to use the bathrooms.

"I know the feeling!" Jack laughed when I told him afterward. Patty, my mom's friend, insisted that Jack talk to her niece because she was now eating gluten-free and felt so much better. She'd also considered the same surgery but had nixed it due to the associated risks. He reached out to her, and she was beyond helpful; she e-mailed him her doctors' names plus her grocery list of what she bought to help ease the symptoms.

Within a matter of days, Jack's mom was out buying gluten-free foods, and he said he felt much better. She suggested acupuncture and certain vitamins, but there was only so far he wanted to take things. He then went into the city with his parents and met with a holistic doctor who didn't take insurance and charged a pretty penny for his time.

Summer moved full speed ahead, and I started to feel neglected. Jack wasn't keeping me in the loop, and many times when I was over at his house, I heard him and his family talking about a doctor's visit I didn't even know he had. I always offered to go with him, but he never took me up on the offer; his mom always went with him. He was going to different hospitals to meet with surgeons, and before I knew it, he set a date with a well-respected surgeon in the city for this surgery.

"What about trying the holistic diet Patty's niece was helping you follow?" I cried.

He said, "Katrina, I want my life back, and this surgery may do that for me."

As with any procedure, there are risks. Jack's doctor warned him that he could become infertile and that his children could still be born with ulcerative colitis one day, even though he wouldn't have it anymore. If the surgery didn't work the way it was supposed to, he would be forced to wear an ostomy bag, which would be attached to his hip, and he would have to empty the feces out himself. The "bag," as Jack called it, could be temporary or lifelong. "If I have to wear that, I will kill myself," was Jack's response.

And if he got an infection, that could also be dangerous. These were pretty heavy conversations for people in their early twenties to be having, and I was terrified. Jack put off applying to graduate school until the second semester, since he'd assumed he would have the first half of the year to recuperate from his late-August procedure.

As July hit, Jack's mom started hitting the bottle hard, often falling asleep on their patio while clutching a glass of Southern Comfort in her hand. He texted me a picture of this one night, and I laughed but also felt the woman's pain. No one ever asked me how I felt regarding Jack's life-changing operation. I was just on the outside looking in as the date inched closer and closer.

One night we came home from the shore, and his mom looked up from the television and announced he had received a phone call earlier in the day from a young man regarding his surgery. Jack knew exactly what she was talking about and nodded; she gave him a note with his contact information written down. We walked into the kitchen, and I asked who the guy was.

"Oh, well, my surgeon spoke to one of her previous patients, who is only a few years older than me, and asked him if he wouldn't mind reaching out to me, to give me some feedback on how his surgery went."

I felt odd all of a sudden—like his mom knew everything about this surgery, including a young stranger calling him, and I was left out in the dark. Was he ashamed to tell me these details? Did he think I wasn't interested? I'm not sure.

Jack called the young man the next day when I was over, and he closed him bedroom door to "talk in private." I sat downstairs on the sofa, sandwiched between his family as they watched the Mets game.

He came downstairs and asked whether I wanted to play some tennis, so as I went upstairs to change into my gear, I asked him how the call had gone. "Fine. It went fine. The guy ended up with the ostomy bag for a few months and had some issues, but now he is completely fine, no side effects. And he even got married and lives a normal life."

I was relieved that Jack had talked to this guy and that his surgeon seemed to really care about him. He was one of her younger patients, and I think that's why she was so helpful. With just weeks away before his "big day," Jack had an awakening.

I was folding laundry one night when suddenly he called me, breaking up our texting conversation as I folded my family's delicates. "Why don't we go to Pittsburgh?" he said, and I burst out laughing. Jack and I had talked about going to Pittsburgh for the past year. Rachel had gone to college there and had stayed after graduation, and Jack's old boss had retired there, and he and Jack had kept in touch with letters and phone calls. He'd even sent Jack a gift for graduation earlier in the summer.

I knew he wanted to see his old boss, and I was dying for a road trip and thought it would be so nice to see Rachel, since the last time I'd seen her was November 2008, when I took the Amtrak train to visit her for a long weekend. Nine hours after waving goodbye to my mom at Newark Penn Station, I was reunited with Rachel in snowy Pittsburgh. We did so much in those three days together and had a great time.

This time around was the middle of July 2012, and this idea made me grin from ear to ear. Jack suggested we go in the next week or so, and he was already looking up hotels. "If you can't go, I was just going to go myself." How romantic.

"No, no, no! I want to go," I said, and I gave him Rachel's phone number so they could coordinate a hotel to stay at and the details. Since the trip was so last minute, she had to work and wasn't able to take off, so we would have some time alone to explore and some time with her. Rachel called me after she got off the phone with Jack (I was now folding bath towels), remarked on how nice he was, and then listed a bunch of hotels. Jack wanted a hotel room (and didn't want to stay in Rachel's tiny studio apartment), because he was afraid of how often he would need to use the bathroom. He said his greatest fear was clogging her toilet or just overusing it in a small space with two girls sitting ten feet away. "No, thank you," he basically said to the idea of staying in her place for free.

The three hotels Rachel recommended to him were either booked or very pricey due to the reservation being the week before. The last one on her list had availability, so Jack just booked it, and he was so cute and booked two beds and a room on the first floor (since I'm terrified of elevators) in case I decided to stay with him.

Then we were all set to go, but I had already been asked to babysit a ton, so our trip was going to be short. I went back and forth with telling the one babysitting mom I couldn't come after all and that something had come up, but I decided against it. I had fun with her two kids, and they were always so good to me. Just the month before, she had given me flowers for my birthday. Jack insisted that it was fine to babysit; he said we would leave on a Wednesday morning and come back on a Friday night. Looking back, I see that the schedule was insane because we were rushed, but it was one of the best trips of my life.

I got to Jack's place bright and early that morning, and he was pacing the house, making sure he hadn't forgotten to pack anything. Instead of a kiss, hug, or handshake, he looked nervous, and my stomach sank. *Here we go*, I thought. *Seven hours in the car, and he is going to be in a crazed mood.* He went to the bathroom as I organized my trunk. I had already stocked the car the night before with water bottles, snacks, napkins, CDs, and hand sanitizer. I went into the house and said hello to his mother, who wished us a nice trip, and then Jack decided he wanted to go to the bathroom "just one more time" before we hit the road.

"Jack, there are tons of rest stops along the way; we aren't heading to Arkansas," I said, gently hinting that we should have been on the road twenty minutes ago.

He came out, and off we went, with him driving my car for the first leg of the road trip. He looked sexy driving my SUV, with his baseball cap on and shorts and a casual T-shirt. "You wanna hear something sick?" he asked as he glided onto the Route 80 West ramp.

"Sure," I said, looking over at the highway entrance, knowing we were officially on our way.

"My aunt called to chat with my mom this morning, who then mentioned the trip to her," he started off. "Then my mom handed me the phone because my aunt wanted to talk to me." I was thinking his aunt (his mom's best friend) was wishing him well on his trip before the surgery. Not exactly. Jack continued, "My aunt said, 'Jack, I understand you booked a hotel room. Whatever you do, don't let her in there! Hotel rooms are for married couples; intimacy is saved for marriage.'"

I burst out laughing but knew that was what his mom and aunt had lost sleep over.

We stopped at a McDonald's to use the bathroom, and even though I'd packed healthy snacks, Jack felt bad we were using the facilities and not buying food, so I took one for the team and purchased a hamburger. As I ate outside my car, the view was so pretty. The rolling hills made this McDonald's appear upscale, and the employees were so friendly it was scary. "People here are so happy to be working at McDonald's; they truly love life," Jack remarked.

I suggested driving as we continued along and entered Happy Valley, also known as the home to all things Penn State. Suddenly, 80 west became very elevated and had only two lanes and no large guardrail, so one slip of the wheel, and you were essentially falling off a cliff. It was drizzling and very gray out all of a sudden, and I was in the left lane and kept glancing over and seeing the barely-there guardrail by the right lane. I was at the beginning of a panic attack.

Tractor trailers blew past us in the right lane as rain suddenly slicked our windshields. I glanced over once more, since I felt my forehead become damp. Jack asked whether I was okay.

"I need to pull over! I'm scared!"

He said, "Not right here, you can't! Get over to the right and go in the shoulder."

I said, "No, that's even closer to the edge!" I proceeded to pull over in the left shoulder, which is reserved for cops in New Jersey. Out here, the roads weren't as populated, and we didn't come across one single state trooper yet. I put my flashers on and felt my knees buckle.

Jack sensed I was freaked out and offered to drive. I said yes, but he told me not to walk around to his side of the car, fearful of a car hitting me. I got into the backseat, and Jack drove me like a chauffeur. I was embarrassed but was honestly terrified of my tires getting too slick and us not being able to stop and going right over the guardrail. Jack pointed out that we were getting close to empty and that we should stop at the next gas station. We had no idea how to pump our own gas, so a man in a pickup truck helped us at a gas station that also moonlighted as a deli. Lovely.

I drove again as the rain came down harder, and the sky became darker the farther west we went. Rachel was working but texted us whenever she could to ask for our whereabouts. Before long, we were in Pittsburgh. It was about seven and a half hours with the rain, and we couldn't wait to get out of the car—that is, if we could ever find the hotel. We punched in the address of the hotel, and my GPS kept announcing, "You have arrived at destination," when we clearly were on a main road, across from a used car dealership and a mini golf place.

I was starting to lose my patience, after we proceeded to go up the same street for the third time, and there still was no hotel. "Are you sure this is a legit hotel? Where is this place?" I cried.

Jack mumbled, "Of course, it's a real hotel—it's a Courtyard Marriot!" And round and round we went again, killing more time. I told him to use my phone and call the front desk to ask for help. He didn't want to (I could hear it in his voice), but he did, and they wound up talking us through it. My stupid GPS never told us to go up to the top of the hill, because once you were up there, you cut across an office building parking lot, and there was the hotel. We checked in, and I ran to open up the blinds to see the view. Well, the view was of the Pennsylvania Turnpike toll booths, so there was nothing too breathtaking. Jack gestured for me to come with him to the hotel lobby shop, since he'd forgotten to bring a toothbrush.

He tossed me his wallet and said to pick out whatever I wanted. I picked out some M&M's and a bag of popcorn, since the room had a microwave. We barely had time to freshen up when the phone rang, and Rachel was on her way. She came to the hotel room, hugged me, and introduced herself to Jack; then she drove us on the scenic route into Pittsburgh (we were apparently staying in the outskirts of town), and at my request, we went to this great restaurant she and I had eaten at during the first time I came to visit.

Dinner was fun, and Jack really enjoyed getting to know her. At one point during dinner, she texted me from across the table, saying, "You guys are too cute!" We walked around downtown afterward, and Jack treated us to frozen yogurt as Rachel mapped out where to go the next day. We hit the hay and were up early the next morning to start our day. It was cloudy and muggy, but the sun was peeking out by the time we posed by the insanely large university campus, sat in a classroom to see what it was like to be in a lecture hall, and bought a ton of souvenirs.

Then I turned to him and said, "You know, West Virginia University is only a little over an hour away from here. Want to go check it out and then come back?"

It was the wildest thing we'd ever done as a couple, and he grinned at me and said, "Sure, let's do it!"

I was already all fired up. It was raining again as we headed to WVU, and we both noticed on a Friday at four o'clock that there was no one in front of us and no one in back of us on this major highway. We were headed to the backwoods of West Virginia, y'all.

We pulled up to the campus, and I already saw more pickup trucks than I care to see ever again. We were dying to buy some WVU apparel, but the bookstore was closed. We toured the campus and then walked downtown, stopping at a cute cupcake shop on the way and picking up some mini cupcakes for Rachel and ourselves. As we left, the sky was raining cats and dogs, and Jack was freaking out as we ran to the car. I asked him what was wrong, and he mumbled something about being worried about getting a disease from running in the rain in flip-flops. He sounded crazy but was really concerned about "dirty rain water" getting on his feet because "Who knows where this water came from?"

We drove downtown and found a college bookstore, so we parked and ran to the door only to discover it was locked, but the sign indicated they were open. We knocked and a young man came to the door and apologized for the sign. His manager had made him do inventory upstairs and he couldn't keep an eye on the cash register at the same time, so he locked the door. He was kind enough to let us shop and then proceeded to leave us alone and went back upstairs. "Just holler when you are ready to pay!" he said.

Was this guy for real? We could have robbed the entire store and headed back to Pittsburgh before he even noticed we were gone. We bought a ton, and he rang us up, and off we went—we wanted to get back into Pittsburgh before dark. We came, we saw, we conquered.

We went to dinner with Rachel, and she later showed us the proper way to pump gas. Jack was teary eyed as we packed, and when I asked why, he said it was because the trip had changed his life; and out of all my friends, he liked Rachel the most.

"She is so honest and real. She is such a good friend."

All these things were true. We left the next morning and drove to a community college an hour outside of Pittsburgh, where his former boss was now working. He hugged us both, and I let him and Jack chat while I roamed the hallways. When we were on our way, I accidently hit "No tolls" on my GPS, so instead of putting us on a main highway, we were the only car going down these eerie, rural streets where all we saw were trailer parks, some of which had outdoor pools. But when we looked closely, we saw that the water in the pools was dirty green. It was very redneck, and I was actually a little nervous and was praying that we would see signs for 80 east sooner than later.

Jack had planned the last day of our trip, and after the college, he signed us up for a tour at Falling Water, a beautiful, famous home-turned-museum. He'd learned about Falling Water in his art class when he was in community college, and he'd thought that since we were out there, we should check it out. It was quite an experience, and we really enjoyed the tour. I called my mom to give her an update on where we were, and I told her we were at "the home of Andrew Lloyd Webber."

Jack laughed and kept saying, "No, no, no! Frank Lloyd Wright designed this house." Whoops.

After we completed our tour, we headed east. We alternated driving most of the trip, but I was tired and wanted Jack to drive. The sky rained on and off the whole way back, and there was nothing out the window but tumbleweeds. We were in the middle of nowhere. We passed signs for the 9/11 memorial in Shanksville, and we wanted to stop, so we thought the next exit was close by. Wrong. We weren't in New Jersey, folks.

The next exit was so far that we thought it was useless to backtrack our way to the memorial. The exit for it had come up too quickly alongside the sign, so we thought if we came upon the next exit, we could easily get off and find it.

"The next time we come out here, we can go there," he said and squeezed my thigh.

The muggy weather was getting to me, as was the constant need to have the wipers on and then off. I have OCD, and this was making me crazy.

"Want to stop for some food?" I asked, just dying to get out of the car for a short while. I punched in "Food" in the GPS because Lord knows we wouldn't have found any places on our own. Lone Star came up, and I hadn't been to one of those in years and had loved going to that steak house with my family on the weekends when it was down the road from my old house. We entered the deserted "rib joint," as my dad used to call it, and I plopped myself into the booth and ordered the messiest, sauciest ribs I could sink my teeth into.

We continued along but stopped off at Penn State to see why so many kids we'd grown up with had chosen that as their place to call home for four years. It was a bit cultlike, and it was even more disturbing when we stopped at a Burger King so I could use the restroom. As I tinkled, I looked up, and a lion stared down at me. Yes, even the Burger King outside the college had the Penn State lion proudly displayed.

We witnessed history because newscasters were outside the school, videotaping students lining up to hug, kiss, and take pictures with a statue of Joe Paterno, the infamous football couch. That was the summer the scandal broke loose, and everywhere you turned, there was another story or allegation being uncovered regarding the school and its beloved coach. We opted not to stand in the rain and take a picture with the statue, but we did take pictures of the people lining up to say good-bye to the statue of the man they'd loved and trusted.

We got back to Jack's around nine o'clock at night and picked up Wendy's right near his house for one last fast-food binge. We chatted with his dad, and then I left to go home. I had to work at the YMCA the next day and should have gotten a sub, but the trip had been pretty spontaneous, and I hadn't had much time. "Next time we do this, I am taking off afterward," I said.

The rest of the summer was fun, with some trips to the beach and nights where we stayed up talking and texting through the wee hours of the morning. "You're my best friend," Jack whispered during a quiet stroll through Hoboken. "I have the most fun when I am with you," he texted late at night, as I read in my bed. "I want you to be the mommy of my children one day because you're such a wonderful human being" was my personal favorite. Jack texted and handwrote cards to me with the sweetest messages. One said, "When I'm with you, I don't care what we do. We could be coloring in a coloring book, and it's fun."

September approached, and it was time for his surgery. The night before his surgery, I desperately wanted to come to his house for dinner, but he didn't extend the offer, and my mom said it wasn't appropriate. "This night is going to be very hard on his family. Let them have a quiet night alone," she said.

Instead I got a haircut and went to a happy hour event hosted by the young professionals group I'd recently joined. I was on edge most of the night, and, looking back, I realize that it was inappropriate for me to be there. As I was exchanging numbers with four girls at the end of the event, I missed Jack's call, and then he texted to say he was going to bed. He had to be in the city at about five o'clock in the morning for his surgery at seven o'clock.

I felt like such a jerk that I'd missed his call and called him back as I drove home. I wished him well and told him I loved him, but I didn't want to make him more nervous than he or his family members already were, so I kept the call short and sweet. I was scared and wished he didn't need this surgery, but I knew it would give him a new lease on life.

The following day, September 11, 2012 was D-day. I woke up, and it was weird not seeing my usual good morning text from him. I was unemployed at the time and had an interview that day at a French school about twenty-five minutes away, so I was preparing for that. When the principal had asked me what day of the week was good, I'd told her Tuesday, hoping it would keep my mind off the day. Maybe it was a sign, but I got the job, and it would go on to be the worst job I ever had. And just as I was being thrown to the wolves at this new school, Jack lay on the operating table.

His parents sent me texts with updates, which meant a lot, since they weren't tech savvy. I threw in a text for good measure to his brother as well, since I knew he must have been nervous. Jack's surgery wasn't completed in one step, as initially thought; he would have a temporary ostomy bag until he could have the second half of the surgery, whenever that would be. I desperately wanted to be there when he awoke, but he also insisted there was no need.

"I will be so out of it from the long surgery that I honestly won't even know who you are." He laughed. When I told this to friends of mine, they just stared at me, confused. But it was what he wanted, and it made sense to me. Instead, I called the hospital that evening and got his room. I was delighted to chat with him, and he sounded out of it, but we had a good twenty-minute phone call. Then I asked Sierra to call as well, except when she did, Jack's father answered, and the nurse came in at the same time, so things got chaotic, and his dad came off as huffy, when in fact he is the nicest man. Jack texted me later on that his parents were "pissing him off," and he couldn't wait until I came.

I went on Thursday with his parents, and what I saw was worse that I'd thought. Jack was in a hospital gown, barely able to walk or sit down. He had an IV hooked up to him as well as a catheter. Memories of my dad rushed to my mind. To this day, the memory I have of that warm September day brings tears to my eyes, and I try to push it away.

I came prepared with my leopard duffel bag full of goodies. I'd stayed up until midnight the night before making him blue Jell-O (something easy to eat), and I'd run out and bought him some magazines and packed the stuffed animal he'd made me for our one-year anniversary. He clutched the bear so much that he wound up putting surgical tape on it. I cut up his meat loaf and tried feeding it to him. I went on to say how delicious it looked, and I how I would eat it too if I was there.

"Oh really? Why don't you?" he said, and I stammered, saying I was full. Hospital food is never appealing, but the Jell-O—it worked like a charm. I also left him some pudding in his small fridge. "Thank God you're here," he said in one moment of silence, without nurses or doctors coming in to check on him. "My parents are driving me insane."

The saddest part of the day came that evening when we were leaving. "Can you stay?" he whispered to me as we hugged good-bye. I had no real plans the next day except getting new brakes on my car and meeting a new family to babysit for. But my mom was out of town, and my car was parked in a parking lot, where his parents had met me that morning. I knew I couldn't leave the car there overnight, and I had no one to go and get it.

"I can't," I said. Looking back, I wish I'd stayed. There were ways to work around getting the car home, but at that late hour, it was hard to find one. He asked me again and again, but I had to go. When I got home that night, I called his brother and asked whether he could take me with him tomorrow to see Jack again. Then I called the babysitting mom, asked to meet her next week, and requested that his brother pick me up at my car dealer, while it sat there all day to get new brakes. I changed my day around for him because I knew deep down that it was the right thing to do.

I spent all day on Friday with him and his brother. I packed playing cards, but he mostly wanted to talk and go for a walk. We helped him and got his IV down the elevator and into the main lobby. It was painful to watch him hobble around, but he enjoyed being in the lobby and seeing people walking about. Jack was discharged that Saturday, a full five days after he was admitted.

I had a wedding to attend that night for an old coworker and asked Derrick to be my date. We had a nice time at the wedding, but I was eager to see Jack the next day. Derrick slept over, and we barely got seven hours of sleep but were up that Sunday morning, baking biscuits, a lasagna, and cookies for Jack and his family. I thought some comfort food from scratch would make his homecoming easier on everyone. After cooking the food, we drove it to his house and visited while he sat in the recliner in his robe. His ostomy bag was how he would go to the bathroom for the time being, and it wasn't easy. It made him very upset, and it was easy to see why. This device was large and was placed on his stomach, but it often leaked and made sleeping or sitting very uncomfortable. He wasn't able to drive for a while, but as soon as he was feeling able to, he made the drive to my house, and we went for a long walk nearby. He looked gaunt and pale; the surgery made it hard for him to digest certain foods, and this problem showed on his face.

Autumn went on, and he was due to have his second surgery, but then he came down with a cold, and they were unable to do it, so it had to be postponed. He had to be in tip-top shape to have it done. So there were more tears and angry words from him, and it seemed that each time I went to his house, he had something negative to say. Our conversations were no longer lighthearted and fun; they had a gloomy theme to them. I was feeling rather doom and gloom myself at that point, and it was only a matter of time before I snapped.

I had been unemployed for eight months and had come down to being the runner-up at two Fortune 500 companies for the positions I'd applied for. I was clearly doing something right to ace the first interviews, but in the end the other person got the job, and I was upset. I sat in traffic three days a week to have French-speaking children throw toys at my head and scream for hours. They never listened and came to school sick, and their parents were no better. I was in a very bad place. Christmas was approaching, and Jack was even angrier than I was, because he now had this ostomy bag for four months, and his second surgery was rescheduled but then canceled again due to his having more complications and getting rushed to the ER one night.

I awoke one morning and saw I had a voicemail from his mother. She assured me that everything was fine, but halfway to the hospital, he realized he'd left his phone at home, so he asked her to call me. Why was this happening to him? Would he never be healthy again? What was wrong with his body at age twenty-three?

We had a nice time around the holidays, but it was tense. Our annual trip to New York City started off with his being in a bad mood because no pants fit him over his "bag," so he had to wear sweatpants. I wouldn't have cared if he wore a banana costume through Times Square, but he got into my car en route to the train station, and the first words out of his mouth were, "I look like a fucking idiot." He was so ashamed to be in sweats, but he wore the nice suede jacket I'd picked out for him the year before, and his hair was nicely done.

We walked slowly through Times Square, bought tickets to see *Elf*, and then made our way over to the tree and then Magnolia Bakery. The final touch of our magical day was riding the Ferris wheel at the Toys "R" Us store in Times Square, which was something I had always wanted to do.

Angelica was having a Christmas party at her apartment right before Christmas, and she lived forty-five minutes past Jack, so I stopped over at his house on the way to the party. He was in a somewhat good mood that evening and offered to walk me to my car after I exchanged gifts with his family. As we sat in my car, he remarked on how nice I looked in my sparkly gold Michael Kors sweater and tight jeans.

"Seeing you all dressed up like this makes me think that maybe you should be out with a guy who's healthy instead of having me drag you down," he suddenly said. His words were so out of left field, but looking back, I see where he was coming from. He'd been invited to Angelica's party, but his mom didn't think it was a good idea for him to be out. I wanted to go, and he told me I should. I called him when I left the party, and he stayed up with me to make sure I didn't fall asleep while driving home.

Christmas came and went, but his bad mood progressed. I tried being positive for him, but his nasty comments outweighed my cheery suggestions. The only upside was that his second surgery was finally slated for the upcoming weeks. A few nights before New Year's, I was going to the movies with a friend and offered to pick him up, but he said no; his mom didn't think it was a good idea to go out. That night or ever? I was confused. He basically said *ever*, because she was worried about the surgery coming up and his catching a cold by being out in public.

Keeping him chained inside his house seemed crazy to me, when he had already been holed up inside there since September, not able to work or see anyone. I was upset and asked him one final time before I went out with my friend. The answer was no, so she and I went. She left around midnight, and he texted me good night but could tell by my tone that I was upset. He called me, and we talked on the phone.

I said I wasn't sure about the relationship anymore and wanted a break. He took this as "I never want to see you again and want to dump you." Truth be told, I was tired of his bitching about anything and everything and I felt that he didn't wanted me around anymore. The last few times I'd been at his house for dinner, everyone had carried on around the table, discussing his medicine, surgery date, and the latest phone call to his doctor; I'd felt like the odd man out. This was the guy who'd always said he couldn't wait to marry me, but now he felt like a stranger.

Since I thought we were just taking some time apart, I wasn't that upset. We tried talking during that week, but he finally said it was too hard to speak to me, and he needed a break. He proceeded to mail me a package with some books I'd lent him as well as our scrapbooks. He cleaned out his room and tossed many of "our things." We started communicating in mid-February, and one cold wintry day, he texted me, "I'm still crazy about you." In March he had his second surgery, and I called him while he was in the hospital and sent him a care package. The only difference was, this time I wasn't at his bedside.

The months went on, and that April we recreated our first date all over again. I rushed home from work to get ready and wanted to look perfect for him. I hadn't seen him since before Christmas, and it now was April 22. He looked different, and it was awkward when it came time to paying, but he paid for my green tea, and we talked for hours. I asked him whether he wanted to go to the Italian restaurant next door, but he said his mom had cooked a big meal; he would just eat at home. It was nine o'clock at night, and I was starving, but he kept insisting that he would just wait for his mom's "big meal." Some things never change.

Then he walked me to my car, we hopped in, and we made out and talked in the dark parking lot for an hour. He came to my house a few nights later, and we went out to dinner, followed by another make-out session. This time I was worried that if we got back together, it would result in marriage, and we both had never really dated anyone else, so I told him that. And he listened.

Before long, we were both going on date after date with losers from the Internet. On one particular dating site, he found me and messaged me, yet we kept going around in circles, with no one making a direct move. We went to lunch near my new office one day in early June, and something was noticeably different about him, but I couldn't put my finger on it. He was texting a lot at the table (something he'd always jokingly yelled at me for doing), and when we parted, he hugged me goodbye, but there was no kiss. Hmm.

A few days later, I almost got into a car accident while pulling into the gym, because Lin and Sierra had both texted me, "Are you and Jack back together?"

I said, no, not exactly. "Why?" I asked, never prepared for what they were about to say.

"It says on Facebook that he is in a relationship," they said, and I felt sick. I texted him real quick to ask whether it was true, and he responded, "Yes, I met someone online, and we made it official last night."

I was sweaty, and my heart raced. "But we made out two weeks ago and kept going out on dates," I stammered.

He wrote back, "I will always love you, but we're not in love anymore."

I went into the locker room, sat on the bench, and cried.

I managed to get myself to kickboxing but cried the whole way home. At one point I cried so hard I could barely see, so I pulled over in a neighborhood I passed every day while going home, but I had never actually been through it. I sat there, staring into space, crying, when suddenly an older man appeared by my window.

"Are you okay?" he mouthed.

I gasped and nodded to show I was fine, and then I was back on my way. I thought about driving into oncoming traffic to stop the pain, but something stopped me. From that night on, I didn't sleep well for two weeks. Every night I tossed and turned, and on many of those nights, I found myself wide awake at four o'clock in the morning, with nothing else to do but read a book in bed, keeping my mind busy until it was time to go to work at nine o'clock.

I was a zombie at the office, barely functioning in my various duties. My eyes were so bloodshot that my coworkers asked whether I had allergies. I lied and said yes. On more than one occasion, I stared at an Excel spreadsheet, not typing, and I suddenly thought of Jack and of how good he always was at Excel. And I remembered that his brother had given me a tutorial in it when I'd had to use it at my last job. I went to the bathroom and cried. I sauntered back to my desk, only to hear my coworker's sixties music channel playing at her desk, with a song repeating over and over: "These eyes ... cry every night for you."

I was falling apart, and it was starting to show. The bags under my eyes made me look like a coke whore. I still dragged my body to the gym each night, but I did my workouts halfheartedly.

I stalked Jack's Facebook and was sickened the more I saw. This girl looked like a hooker. My friends said it, as did my cousins and mother. I had no idea what this hair-extension-using, lingerie-wearing hooker wanted in Jack, but I had a few guesses as to what he saw in her. He barely talked to me, since he was so busy driving over an hour each way to see her and chauffeur her around to state fairs and such. She didn't drive, she smoked like a chimney, and she liked hard alcohol.

The breaking point came when my family went to North Carolina for vacation the week of the Fourth of July. He posted Facebook pictures of them at a pool, ready to have a good time. She wore a patriotic bikini, and he wore a Fourth of July-inspired do-rag (yes, I'm being 100 percent serious); they both looked ridiculous, as Sierra put it. I had about enough. I texted him right then and there (after he had the audacity to text my mom a happy birthday) and asked to see him right when I got back to town. He made up some nonsense that he was so busy with work, but I pushed again and again.

I got back to town, and after much pleading, I got him to come to my office later that week for "lunch." We sat outside on a hot bench; I cried, and he asked why he was there. I handed him a typed, two-page letter detailing my feelings for him, and he left. Later that night he texted me that he'd found a movie stub in the shorts he wore that day; the stub was from a movie we saw the summer before, and I knew it was a sign. I told him so, and he agreed.

Two days later he dumped that girl but wanted to clear his head before jumping back into a relationship with me. We went to New York City later that August and had the best time eating deli sandwiches on the High Line and buying tickets to the World Trade Center Memorial. The next day he told me he loved me.

"You mean it?" I said, and then we agreed to try dating again. We wanted to see how graduate school would be for him, since he knew his program would be grueling. Sure enough, it *was* grueling, and he was never around. We took a weekly dancing class and had the best time each week. Looking into his eyes as we danced the fox-trot and waltz was magical; I liked how we were the youngest students in the class, yet he always found time to chat with the teacher and his wife. His mannerisms were old fashioned, and I told my mom, "After all this time, I still get butterflies when I look at him."

That autumn was brutal. Despite my baking him cookies for his "one year of being healthy anniversary" and doing everything I could to prove I was "wife material," he was conflicted and was unsure about dating me again, saying it would "most likely result in marriage," and he wasn't sure whether we were meant to be married. He kept bringing up our differences, and I agreed we had some, but so did everyone.

"I think I need to be with someone I have more in common with" was the type of statements he made. I cried over him all the time. I was the one who'd started this mess the year before, but he took it to a whole other level. A few weeks before Christmas, I sat on the couch at the house where I was babysitting, staring at their tree and playing a sad Miley Cyrus song on repeat, when I decided it would be a good idea to call Jack. He answered and said he was playing video games with his brother, so he couldn't chat much. He texted me later that night and said that "it was so good to hear my voice," and my stomach churned, and I felt sick. I still didn't think he wanted me back, but I was determined to change his mind.

Right around Christmas, he came to my office for lunch and asked me out again. "We are going to have a great life together. I just know it," he said to me, after stating that my note in the Christmas card I'd handed him had made him cry. I had written that I was sorry for my actions the year before and would take them back if given the opportunity.

"Will you accept my courtship?" he asked, and I did, but I wanted to discuss some details first, so the mistakes we'd made the first time around didn't happen again. Yet he turned things around and basically took back his offer. Unreal.

New Year's rolled around, and he called me and said we needed to end things once and for all. There would be no proposal on the beach, no honeymoon to "somewhere warm" with the passport I'd helped him get, and no set of twin children. He said our families were too different, and he needed to "see what else was out there" and encouraged me to do the same. So I did.

Then one cold January night, after I came back from a really great date, I was gushing to my mom about it and then went to sleep. I received a late-night text from Jack. "Hey—are you still up?" He'd unblocked my number; this must be important.

I said no; I was sleeping. "Is everything okay?"

He had the nerve to say he missed me and that he was thinking of "us." Then a few days later, we argued again over my wanting a relationship but his still saying we weren't meant for each other, and he blocked me again, and that was that. Or so I thought.

The spring months rolled in, and he would e-mail or text me, only to block me again when I made him "angry" with something I'd said. He said we fought too much, which I said wasn't true. I cried over him for months.

To this day, he is still the second person (after Sierra, of course) to wish me a happy birthday, and he still wishes me a merry Christmas. The movie *Dirty Dancing*, which was always a favorite of mine, now had new meaning, because it was the movie we'd watched on the night we had our first make-out session, and it was also the movie we'd watched the last time I ever stayed over at his house. There is a line in the movie, which Baby says to Johnny, that reminds me of Jack: "I'm scared of everything. I'm scared of what I did, of who I am … And most of all, I'm scared of walking out of this room and never feeling the rest of my whole life the way I feel when I'm with you." *

*"Dirty Dancing," directed by Emile Ardolino (1987; Great American Films Limited Partnership), DVD.

I wonder whether I will ever feel the same way about someone else that I felt about him. Sierra and my mom say no; they say you never truly forget the magic and memories of a first love. Anyone else who comes after it is sort of second best, I feel.

Although I'd never fully comprehended how hard dating could be, I learned it firsthand in the months following Jack. I tried online dating six months after being apart from him, and it was no picnic. The first guy who messaged me was nice until he corrected my grammar, made fun of my friends, and called me a liar. I never felt as sick as I did when I pulled into the park in town to meet him on the hottest day in June.

We agreed to "shoot hoops" on our first date, because we both liked basketball. Well, I came there dressed in a casually nice outfit, and he came, well, dressed to shoot hoops. He was very serious about the rules of "Horse," and I felt he was mocking me when I didn't get shots in.

"I thought you said you liked basketball," he said, and I felt my blood pressure rise. As time went on and we decided to sit in the shade and get to know each other, I told a story and used my real name to refer to myself, and he cut me off and said, "I thought your name was Kat?" And I said that yes, people call me that (and on the online dating profile I had put that as my name), but my real name is Katrina. He looked me dead in the eye and said, "What else have you lied to me about?" Let's just say we never had a second date.

Then I had a date with a garbage man, who after twenty minutes of sitting across from me at the restaurant wanted to marry me. I didn't know he was a garbage man; he told me he worked in the recycling industry but was "upper management." "Yes, meaning he drives the truck instead of picking up the garbage cans!" Sierra exclaimed.

Needless to say, the minute I sat down and saw him, I felt sick. He had chest hair peeking out of his sweater, he was going slightly bald, and he was boring. He kept tossing out the words *upper management* and talking about his job, which I had no knowledge of; and when I tried to ask questions, he went into such deep detail that I found myself staring at the picture on the wall above his head, mentally going over my grocery list. The only way to end this nightmare was to hit the bathroom and then compose myself and say I needed to leave, since I had a family dinner later that evening. That wasn't a total lie, but I did want to hit the ShopRite near the restaurant to get menstrual pads, toothpaste, and a few other items.

I told him I needed to head out to get to my aunt's, and then he said, "Oh, but I thought you were heading there at seven. It's only five thirty." I said, yes, but I needed to pick up a dessert first at ShopRite. A bit of a lie.

"Oh, I see. Mind if I came with you, and we walked and talked more in the store? I feel like I could talk to you all night," he said.

I stammered and said that was very kind of him, but no, I needed to get the cake and go, because I also needed gas. He paid, and we walked outside, and he remarked on what a nice car I had. "Mind if I take a look inside?" he asked.

I didn't know what to say, so I muttered, "Sure." But then my stomach sank as I looked around the dark parking lot and saw not a soul. I wondered whether this was a ploy to throw me in the backseat, drive me somewhere, and kill me. If it had been, boy, was he good.

It turned out that he really did just like cars. "You have a lot of mileage. You drive a lot?" he asked, and I realized I'd had just about enough fun for one evening.

This fun escapade didn't end there. He kept texting me until I couldn't fake it any longer. I said I was still "missing my ex-boyfriend and didn't think dating was a good idea right now." That's wasn't a total lie, but I was also still online (different website) talking to other guys, but I just had no intention of seeing this guy again.

"Are you sure you don't want to give us another try? I think we have great potential," he said, making it only so much worse. I kept insisting that no, my feelings weren't going to change, and I was so sorry. He was a great guy, blah-blah.

Then, a few nights later, I was baking in the kitchen when I suddenly got a phone call from a blocked number. *Hmm, that's weird,* I thought. My hands were in dough, but I never planned on picking up anyway. When I told a good friend the next day, she said, "You know it was him, don't you? Katrina, he sounds crazy!" And I knew deep down that it most likely *was* him. Well, he never called again or begged me to reconsider him again, and that was that.

Then came Joe. He was hot, fun, and hilarious. He said the fact that I packed a lunch every night in a lunch box for work was "adorable." The first phone conversation we ever had was an hour long, and afterward he texted me: "The only time I've ever been on the phone that long in the past was with Verizon, and this was way better" with a smiley face. He texted me every morning and every evening, and then we agreed to meet up at a bar/restaurant in town to have drinks and watch a Jets game. He was hotter than I thought, and apparently Sierra's brother thought so too, because he worked there and came over to our table to say hi. He told her, when he got home, that I was out with a "good-looking dude."

While the date went seemingly well, I found it concerning when he knocked back four beers in the course of two hours and was texting at the table. I got annoyed and said, "Oh, if you need to get that, you can."

He replied, "Oh, sorry; it's fantasy football time, and my cousin is texting me about our picks." Huh, well, that's polite, isn't it? I should have gotten up and left, but I stayed.

Our second (and last) date was a few weeks later at our favorite bar/restaurant in our college town. We'd not only grown up in the towns next to each other but also gone to the same college; we both played sports and had the same favorite restaurant. On that night, he knocked back four beers again and then proceeded to hit the bathroom after he stumbled off the bar stool. I asked whether he was okay to drive home. He said, "Oh yeah, it's a straight shot down 287—you know that."

I cringed and stopped myself from giving a speech on how buzzed driving is drunk driving. As he came back, he asked whether I wanted to smoke outside with him, and I just stared at him. He winked. "You know, a cig?" I said no, and then he laughed and said he was "just kidding." And then he proceeded to tell me a story that ended with his using the words "my dick." I realized I was done. And I needed to leave. Like now.

He asked where I'd parked, and I pointed a few rows over and said, "Over there." He said he was a few rows "that way." We did an awkward, ass-out hug, and off we went. That was the end of Joe.

And then there was Pete. His dating profile showed him posing with his dad at a Giants game in matching jerseys, grinning from ear to ear. I thought he was a family man, so I liked that angle. Then in his profile, which asked what books he liked, he'd written, "I don't read books." I'd looked past that detail and considered giving him a try; he lived in the town where I worked and had grown up twenty minutes north of me. I was due to meet him a few weeks into the winter season, and the night of our date happened to be a state of emergency snowstorm, so I asked him to postpone it until the following week. I wasn't going to work, let alone go out to meet some guy, when our governor had told us to stay the "hell off the roads."

Then on the day of our date, he texted me, asking whether we were still on and wrote, "Let's hope this time you don't cancel again." I kindly replied that if the weather was safe and we aren't expecting twelve inches of snow again, he could count on me to show up. And I did, and we had fun. He was cute and charming, and we had two hours of great conversation. And then he paid, and we got out to the parking lot. He took out his keys and gestured to his black Hyundai right in the front.

"Wow, you got prime parking! I parked way in the back next to a mountain of snow." I laughed and gestured down the dark parking lot to where my car was parked.

"Oh, tell me about it; there is snow everywhere!" he said, and we did that awkward, ass-out hug good-bye, and I never heard from him again. I texted him and thanked him, and he told me to have fun at my kickboxing class the next night, and that was it. Poof! He was gone.

The last two guys I had online dates with made me realize I'd hit rock bottom. The first was a Muslim guy who kept telling me he was online looking for his "Princess." During our date, he told me a story about his sex life and then told me about his family and their strict views on dating and religion. Then he asked me about my views on religion.

"Oh, so you're a good Catholic girl, are you?" He smirked. As we started to leave the coffee shop, I mentioned my car was parked far, yet he had a front row spot, so he proceeded to say good-bye to me. Clearly I was going to walk to my car alone, in the dead of winter, again.

"I don't know if I feel a connection. What do you think?" he called out as I was turning to walk off into the night. I agreed that I felt nothing and was relieved when I said it aloud, but then I was upset that my sister had spent so much time straightening my hair and doing my makeup. I was also pissed; I now had to watch *The Bachelor* On Demand because I'd missed it for being with this Saudi Arabian "prince" for an hour. Yes, an hour. (The more you date, the quicker you realize how long you are willing to tolerate someone. In his case, it was one hour on a Monday night.)

He later texted me a picture of his Spanish friend, asking whether I "liked him." "He lives forty-five minutes from you but is a good Catholic boy—you guys would get along great!"

I said, "No, thank you." And that was it, until Friday night. As eleven thirty rolled around, he texted me, "Heyyyy." I never replied. What a sicko.

Then came Ray. Ray was number eight of my horrible dates and my last one for ten months. I needed a break after him. A long one. He said he was an English teacher and lived in my family's town, which didn't make much sense, because the area of town he lived in had multi-million-dollar homes, and as a teacher, I didn't believe his salary typically included multiple commas. Then he proceeded to tell me he was also "vice principal" at the school (he never told me which school, just the "county" it was in), and in the summer he also taught English as an adjunct professor at the university he'd graduated from, which happened to be next to the one I went to. I thought it was odd that he could be a teacher *and* vice principle at the same time, and he was twenty-six but owned a house in an affluent part of town.

I googled him and tried multiple ways to dig up anything on him: the school where he taught, his adjunct teaching job in the summer, and his tax records on the house he supposedly owned. Nothing came up. And I was crafty with my searches too. I should have known, but I agreed to meet the kid anyway. I say the word *kid* because he showed up at that same upscale bar/restaurant where I'd seen Joe a few months before, wearing white tennis sneakers, light-colored jeans, and an ugly Christmas-type sweater. He also had braces on.

"I'm on a date with Doogie Howser, MD, right now" I texted my friends after I snuck off to the bathroom. "Remember *Sixteen Candles*?" I wrote to Jo Jo. "Well I'm on a date with Anthony Michael Hall's character from that movie now." This guy was *that bad*. I wish I were being dramatic, but that was my lowest point yet. In his profile pictures, he looked completely normal but those must have been old photos. Or they'd been photoshopped. On top of all of this, he ate like a slob; and when the bill came, I offered to pay (for mine), and he took me up on it.

I realized in that moment that God was playing a very cruel joke on me. He was testing me to see just how far I would go to find love. And I wasn't willing to go that far; I wasn't *that* interested in dating and falling in love. I told myself I wasn't dating again for a very long time. Then ten months later, Dan appeared.

Now, Dan, as you see, was someone I had heard about my entire life. Jo Jo worked with his mother, and his name had been mentioned since I was a junior in high school. Having grown up in the town next to him, I often asked Jo Jo whether maybe I had seen him out somewhere, like at the movies. "I don't think he goes out a lot," is what she always said.

When I was sixteen and looking for a date for the junior prom, she mentioned Dan and borrowed a picture from his mother. "He has an afro!" I said, shook my head, and told her, "Thanks but no thanks."

Fast-forward years later. Jo Jo still mentioned him and where he went to college, and I felt like I somehow knew him. Well, after Dan and his girlfriend broke up, his mom mentioned the idea of setting us up to Jo Jo. She asked me what I thought, and I realized I was *much* more comfortable with being set up with someone carefully selected and highly recommended by a trusted family member than with someone I'd met over the Internet. We all saw how well that turned out, didn't we?

She passed along a few photos of me, and immediately he texted me, asking me out for that Friday night. Now, I was having a Christmas party at my condo that Saturday night and had a ton to do. I wanted to clean, do laundry, bake, and cook. I wanted to make the guest room upstairs ready for my two friends who were sleeping over, and I was aiming to stay in and do this all on Friday night. I expressed this to Jo Jo and mentioned that Christmas was the following week, and I was feeling rushed, with gifts to wrap and food to bake. This timing was just bad.

She said he was leaving for Florida to visit his grandma, and if I wanted to postpone our date, I should, but then it wouldn't be for almost two weeks since he was going away. I pondered this, and against my better judgment, I asked my friends, and they all told me to just go that Friday night, because "he may lose interest in two weeks." He texted me a time and place, and I got myself in tip-top shape that week. He said he "couldn't wait for our date," and I felt myself start to perspire.

I got waxed (no one likes a lady with a mustache), tried on every outfit in my closet until I found a suitable one, and bought some new makeup. I didn't sleep at all that week. Every night I tossed and turned and found myself waking up anxious. The thought of another date after my eight awful ones scared me, and the ten months I had taken off from dating were so wonderful. I was scared to blow it by making date number nine another bum one. I was so tired all week long that I was running on empty at the gym and found myself too anxious to eat. I got on the scale and was down three pounds. Dan was making me lose my mind, and I hadn't even met him yet.

On the night of our date, I met him at the bar/restaurant where I'd had my first date with Joe; this time we sat at the table next to the booth where Joe and I had sat. At first glance, I thought he was handsome. I found myself noting his shoes, sweater, and jeans; his dress was practical, but he had expensive taste.

He started off with, "Well, how did you get roped into this?" and I laughed. My weeklong nerves were lifted, because before long, we were eating, drinking, laughing, and having a great time. It felt so easy to talk to him; the connection just felt natural. I looked at him and felt a sense of peace, like God was finally doing me a favor after putting me through eight dates with guys who were pigs and didn't treat me how a lady deserves to be treated. I felt like this was finally it. Thank You, Jesus!

The date went on for three hours, and I looked him up and down for signals that he wanted to leave or for me to stop talking. But he was the talker. The date flowed, and at no point did things turn weird or reach a point when I wanted to leave. I felt as comfortable as I had during my first date with Jack all those years ago. *Good things come to those who wait*, I told myself. I excused myself and headed to the bathroom. When I returned, he paid and then continued to smile at me across the table until I was fighting back yawns; at that point he asked whether I was ready to go.

We headed outside and started to walk up the hill leading to our cars, and that's when things became weird. "Well, I'm right here," he gestured, fiddling with his car keys. I thanked him for a great night and mentioned that I was parked up the hill. We did the awkward ass-out hug, and I said I would love to do this again, and he looked me in the eye and agreed. He said he would call me the next day, and I turned to walk up the dark street (alone again in the dead of winter), and the night was over.

I went home and sat on my mom's bed as Lin asked me for all the details. I couldn't help beaming from ear to ear. My friends were all texting, and so was Jo Jo, and they all said the same thing: "This finally seems like the right one for you."

Then I never heard from Dan again—not the next day, like he said, or the day after that. So I texted him, and right off the bat, his texts were odd and unfriendly. Then again, we'd really never texted to begin with, so I'm not sure how he was with texts. And come to think of it, at the restaurant I never saw him on his phone once, not when he was waiting for me to arrive or when I was coming out of the bathroom. Maybe he wasn't a phone guy. I tried hard to read between the lines of his texts, but he would write back twelve hours later, and that's when the writing was on the wall.

This guy had played me for a fool. Not only had he wasted my Friday night by leading me on, but he'd also wasted my Friday night a week before Christmas and the night before my holiday party. I'd had a million things to do, but I'd given them up to meet him, and how had he paid me back? By being a jerk. Maybe he'd been heartbroken over his ex-girlfriend, maybe he'd seen me as a rebound, or maybe he'd just seen me as "fat friend material." I will never really know.

I cried in the shower twice that week and found myself angry and bitter during Christmas, while people around me were happy and "in love." I hate to say Dan ruined my Christmas that year, but he did. I should have listened to my gut and gone out with him after the holidays after things had quieted down, but I listened to everyone else around me. In the future I will know to listen to me; guys have treated me like crap for years, and guess what? They can wait. I'm not dying to get married, nor am I dying for a date. There are too many desperate women out there, and I'm not one of them. I act like me and tell real stories, and if you don't like it, there's the door. In Dan's case, he seemed to like my stories and how "real" I was.

I have never felt so low in my life than during the weeks that followed his blowing me off. Jo Jo was floored, and so were my friends, and then I told myself to forget him and the whole night. Forget I ever met him and wasted three hours of my time with him. If three hours of great conversation by two people, whom family had set up and who had grown up five minutes from each other, weren't enough to make this work, then I clearly had nothing to offer the opposite sex.

I then remembered a night when Jack and I went to Hoboken to have dinner, and as we strolled past the water, couples sat on benches and stared at the bright lights of the city just across the Hudson. As we walked past one couple, the guy stared me up and down while his date sat there. I noticed him do it, but I didn't think Jack did. Oh, he did it all right and made some crack that if we ever broke up, some guy would swoop me up in no time. A similar occurrence took place the day we went bike riding and a jogger stopped to warn us about a huge turtle up ahead that was blocking the path. The guy told me all about the turtle and then proceeded to tell me that I "really should be careful" and so forth, while Jack just stood next to me, being totally ignored.

"Who the hell did that guy think I was? Your brother?" he spat out while I just cracked up, but he didn't find it quite as hilarious as I did. I suppose I thought instances like that meant I was attractive and that guys clearly wanted to converse with me. My cousins always tell me I'm attractive, and my friends and coworkers rave about some of my outfits. Am I maybe imagining these compliments? No, I don't think so.

I sometimes wonder if perhaps I'm not really as attractive as I think I am. Do I look like Shrek, and no one is kind enough to tell me? For years I hated how I looked, and apparently so did all the boys I knew. Nowadays I look completely different and feel more confident than ever, but I still tend to meet losers without manners or real jobs. So either I'm just not as hot as I perceive myself, or I'm just looking for a mate in all the wrong places.

The mere thought of another date with a stranger makes me feel sick. "The forced awkward, intimate situation (as they say in The Wedding Crashers) isn't romantic or fun, and neither is the waiting game afterward. "Is he going to call? He said he was going to call!" is a game that hurts and makes my anxiety rise. I'm checking my phone so often that I think it must be broken, because guess what? He never called after he said he would. Or he did call or text, but he doesn't sound as fun or cheery as he did on your date, so you wonder, *Does he even still like me?* And in some cases, you go on a second date with him, only to realize that maybe he isn't as fun as he was on the first date and actually has awful manners and stinky breath.

It's all one big game, and I'm being completely honest when I say I want no part of it. When I was an overweight teenager with bushy hair and braces, every year I wished for two things when blowing out the candles on my birthday cake: for Nick Carter to marry me one day or for me to get a boyfriend. And I'm still hoping Nick Carter comes around. The other wish? If it happens, it happens.

Lasagna

As my mom likes to tell it, I was born hungry. While some people choose to worship the bottle, I chose to worship our food pantry. From the time I was an infant to the time I was a high school senior, the same discussion always came up during my yearly physical. "Katrina is such a good eater!" The first time a doctor ever said this to my mom, I was an infant.

She replied, "Well, I give her one bottle, and then she is still hungry, so she cries. So I give her more!" Sigh. I was always hungry.

Imagine growing up as the only overweight girl in your entire class. Now, I wasn't raised in the outskirts of some sleepy North Carolina town or in the backwoods of West Virginia. I was raised in northern New Jersey, where the majority of the population works in New York City and is up to date on the latest trends and fashions. I could sit and try to grasp why I was targeted for looking a certain way, but I may be sitting a long time. Was it because I couldn't fit into the hip clothes my peers were wearing? And that Abercrombie & Fitch was just a store I passed by in the mall and didn't even consider going into, because a sales associate would have snarled a remark similar to the one in *Mean Girls*. "Sorry, we only carry sizes one, three, and five … You could try Sears."

Who knows? What I do know is that back when I was young and literally had more rolls on me than a bakery, people were mean. Whether it was my own peers, the boys I had crushes on, or my gym teachers, I was constantly a target. And I was a shy girl who never spoke up in class, and I longed to fit in.

Food was tasty, and I always wanted more of it. In the first grade, we had a Girl Scout event, and we got to eat at Pizza Hut as a reward. The long table was filled with twenty Girl Scouts and a few leaders. I was at one end of the table, and when it was time to leave, I remember walking out and seeing that all the plates on the table were only half eaten. I wolfed down my personal pan pizza, but apparently no one else did.

To this day I remember wanting to eat some of their food as I walked past the plates, thinking what a shame it was that little girls could be so wasteful. In all seriousness, I could have eaten their crusts and leftover slices, but I knew it was poor taste to even ask such a question. But how on earth could you not finish four small slices of pizza? I would ask myself the same questions all throughout elementary school when friends were "too busy" to finish their lunch or snacks, being too excited to go outside. I was as excited to climb our jungle gym as the next guy but not until after I'd finished my lunch.

The earliest memory I have of being "different" (and by this, I mean overweight) was when I was in the second grade. Having grown up as a tomboy, who was always chosen to be on the boy's team in kickball, basketball, and volleyball, I was invited to boys' birthday parties. One particular birthday party that comes to mind was a roller skating party for a boy in my class; only two girls in the whole grade were there. I had a blast skating around the roller rink until the announcement came that it was time for lunch. I wiggled a spot on the bench next to the only other girl there and dug into my slice of pizza. Then it started. The birthday boy had two popular older brothers, and suddenly one of them said, "Katrina is taking up the whole bench!" Immediately everyone around me erupted into laughter.

Even at seven years old, I was wise and thought that if I chose to ignore their cruel taunts and just talked to the girl next to me, they would stop. That's what they teach us in school, isn't it? If you're getting bullied, ignore your attacker, and eventually he or she will stop. Wrong. Always fight back, regardless of what teachers and guidance counselors tell you. Instead of reaching for a second slice of pizza like everyone else, I sat there in silence until my mom came to pick me up. I can still remember her arriving, and I ran and pulled on her sleeve to get me out of there. The party mother walked over to me just as I was about to make my escape.

"Katrina, don't forget your goody bag! Thanks so much for coming today!" I took the goody bag and sat in silence the rest of the car ride home.

It was especially cruel when all the cool girls in my grade started to wear jeans and fun tops, but those clothes weren't exactly available in the plus-sized section of the store where I shopped. There's a picture of me perched atop the highest bleacher (for the taller kids) when I was in the fifth grade, and in the chorus concert picture, I'm wearing a fuzzy, green turtleneck. I really loved that turtleneck and wore it quite often. Years later I found the shirt in my closet, pushed way in the back, and discovered it was a size 1X from the misses department. I was eleven years old. I typically wore an XL top and size 13 or 14 pants, which was pretty extreme. I wasn't just "big boned," and it wasn't just "baby fat." I had an addiction to food, and I was never going to simply "grow out of it."

The rest of my elementary school career consisted of me hanging out with Rachel and Sierra, and despite looking different from other kids, I had no desire to change. Then, during the summer before middle school, my mom told me a story. When she was growing up, every summer some of the heavy girls came back to school thinner in September. So I decided I wanted that too. It was the first diet I ever went on, but believe me, it wasn't the last one by any means.

I started getting up every morning at ten o'clock (I've always loved my sleep just as much as my food), and after eating breakfast, I walked our entire circular driveway. My mom told me to pump my arms "to get rid of arm jiggle," so I incorporated that in too. Then I went inside for lunch and baked five, breaded, dinosaur-shaped chicken nuggets in the toaster oven and toss them into a salad. All the while, I thought I was being sophisticated, because grown-ups ate chicken in their salads. I didn't realize that grown-ups ate *grilled* chicken in their salads, not breaded chicken shaped like carnivores. Then I chopped up some lettuce and tomatoes, diced some full-fat cheddar cheese, and tossed that in—and are you ready for this? I poured extra-virgin olive oil around the entire salad until it was dripping. I should have just consumed an entire jar of mayonnaise for lunch; it would have saved me the time it took to chop everything.

I thought my meal was beyond healthy. And once a week my mom and I did errands and passed a Wendy's on our route, so she treated us to lunch. I was trying so hard to stick to my diet and therefore would order a small order of french fries and a side salad with bleu cheese dressing. I didn't know it was the worst possible dressing (as far as fat content) that a person could order. So, as you can imagine, the scale didn't exactly budge that summer. Or the summer after that.

Middle school was brutal and not kind to overweight teenagers with bushy hair and braces. We honestly had no overweight kids in my entire grade, except me and this one boy. During a field trip only a few months before, he was made fun of as he tried to climb onto a horse at the ranch. "He's going to break the horse!" screamed one of the boys in my grade, and everyone burst into laughter.

The boy got off the horse and cried, while everyone else rode off into the sunset. I repeated this story to my mom later that evening, and she remarked, "You kids are getting so mean these days." And it was 1998, and yet that was such a true statement. Kids have only gotten worse. The boy who made the rude comment at the ranch was never seen from again after eighth grade. Rumor has it that he went to a juvenile detention center. What goes around comes around.

My first memory of junior high wasn't warm and fuzzy, although it was a warm and sunny day. My mom walked me down our driveway just as the bus was pulling up. Just like I'd done all throughout elementary school, I waved to her from my window once I found a seat. Unlike elementary school, the girls on the bus were dressed like baby prostitutes, with push-up bras bubblegum-pink lipstick, and heavily sprayed-on perfume. As I looked around, taking all this in, one of the boys in my grade had a sudden interest in my Spice Girls T-shirt.

"Which one are you? Fatty Spice?" he asked, while all the guys around him roared with laughter. I sat there, sweating profusely, and said nothing.

As you can imagine, I dreaded getting on the bus. The bus was the main problem I had with being bullied, because all the trouble began on the bus. And that was only at seven thirty in the morning. The bus drivers never stepped in to intervene, not even when a quiet boy in my grade had nowhere to sit. All the boys in my grade argued, "He isn't sitting with me; he's a loser!" and so forth. No one would let him sit, and he was the last stop, so seats were limited at that point. The non-English-speaking bus driver did nothing but tell him to sit down, and eventually he did—on the floor of the bus.

When the bus driver told him to get up, he still had nowhere to go. So an eighth grader, who lived down the block from him, grabbed the ringleader by the shirt collar and told him that if he didn't "shut the hell up and move in," she was going to "kick his ass." Well, that solved the problem real fast. The boy had a seat, but all was still not well. He ended up leaving our middle school shortly after that and returned in high school. I heard he'd transferred to a Catholic school nearby. I would have loved to switch schools myself.

Gym class in middle school was also a nightmare. Unlike the fun days of gym class twice a week in elementary school, middle school physical education required a uniform and was a daily occurrence. I still cringe thinking about how every fall and spring the teachers would take us outside, line us up, and shoot us. No, actually they would line us up, blow the ridiculous whistle around their necks, and time us as we "ran the mile." I was always the last person to finish. I would round the bend just as the teachers were packing up their clipboards to head inside, so we could all change and head to our next classes (sweaty as hogs because the showers didn't function properly). My typical time for the four laps (one-mile run) was 13:30, although as the years went by, I got it down to 11:30. But the teachers insisted that the girls had to finish in less than ten minutes and boys in less than seven. So I was way off, as you can see. Then I got crafty, and as time went on, I "forgot" my gym uniform on the days we practiced the mile.

"It must be in the laundry basket at home!" I exclaimed. It was better to take a zero and sit on the bleachers than to be the heaviest person out there, chugging along as everyone zipped past me. I couldn't even finish one lap around the track without stopping. I was completely winded, short of breath, and wanted to just fall over and die. And when the mile was completed, I collapsed on the bench in the locker room, unable to get up. The teachers gave us only a few minutes to change, so you can imagine, by me sprawling out on the bench for the first two minutes, that it was a rushed escapade.

Although I was carrying an extra fifty pounds, I was good at some sports. I was a dynamo in volleyball, and the boys always picked me to be on their team. I could hold my own in basketball too, getting in multiple shots as we played in gym class. The boys in my seventh-grade gym class liked me due to my athletic ability, and this carried over into the rest of my classes that year, since most of the same students were in my classes due to the "team" we'd landed on.

But I still wanted to fit in and be pretty. I had braces on, but my mom let me pick out makeup that year, and I had some semi-hip clothes. Still, it was hard to fit into the tight jeans all the girls in my grade were wearing. I was embarrassed each year as we lined up to pick out our new gym uniform, since I had to walk up single file and tell the three-hundred-pound male gym teacher what size shirt and shorts I needed. "I'll take an extra-large top and large shorts, please," I muttered quietly. A noisy girl in my grade sometimes asked why I changed in the cramped bathroom stall. I brushed off her question and said it was because "I felt like it."

I'm all for surprises, but one surprise I always hated. One day each year in gym class, the teachers announced we weren't going outside; instead we were going to have the "push-up and sit-up test." On this day, the teacher called us up one by one and made us do as many push-ups as we could while he or she held a stopwatch; the rest of the class sat in their assigned spots in the gym (alphabetical order in rows) and watched us.

The teacher made us touch our chins to a hockey puck. To anyone who has ever attempted this, it is nearly impossible. I'm just going to put that out there. The first time they tried this stunt with us in sixth grade, my body collapsed and hit the ground after I did one push-up. The teacher actually looked embarrassed when he whispered for me to go back and sit in my seat.

The sit-up test wasn't quite so awful, because a few of us were called up one at a time and were able to choose a partner to "hold our feet" while we did the sit-ups. My partner always gave me a few extra sit-ups for good measure when it was time to tell the teacher how many we had done, and he or she wrote the number down on his or her little clipboard. As I walked back to my row, I always caught this one boy in my grade smirking at me. I knew he was mocking me for being so out of breath from a few sit-ups and not being able to do more than one push-up. I just walked back to my seat as fast as I could.

There's another day I dreaded in middle school gym class. It was the once-a-year occasion when the female teacher lined us girls up in the locker room in just our bras and shorts, and checked our spines for scoliosis. When it was my time to step right up, she had me bend over to the floor and touch my toes while she traced the outline of my spine. I used to clutch my T-shirt in my hands and shield it over my body so I wasn't as exposed. Looking around at the other girls in their tiny bras with their baby six-pack abs made me envious. I wore a C-cup bra and carried fifty pounds on them. Yet when it came down to lunch in the cafeteria, they were the ones eating pizza and french fries every day, while I had a nicely packed lunch made courtesy of my mom. Yet I was the heavy one.

You know that saying, "Children say the darndest things"? Children also say the rudest things. That was the case of this little brat in Pennsylvania I helped babysit when I was staying with Rachel for a few days in the summer before eighth grade. Rachel's new neighborhood in suburban Pennsylvania was very nice, and this house was just like the rest. It had a large front yard and a marble kitchen, and two sprawling staircases greeted you upon entering. That same house in New Jersey would have easily cost $800,000.

We walked over, and the mom was running out the door to head to a workout class she taught, and within a quick glance around the house, I saw more Jane Fonda workout videos and dumbbells than I ever had in my life. She was pretty, in good shape, and heavily done up for the middle of the morning in the summer. Her only child was about five years old, and she sauntered downstairs, and we played some games and made her lunch. She insisted on eating only an olive oil sandwich, which Rachel and I both politely told her wasn't happing. She insisted some more, and Rachel kept telling her no; she would get a stomachache.

I had never babysat before, so I just quietly stayed out of it. Then a short while later, as we sat on the carpeted living room floor, playing a game, I announced I was headed to the bathroom and would be right back. Then I heard it. I was halfway down the hallway when I heard the little bitch (I mean, brat) say, "Why is your friend so fat?"

I stopped in my tracks (I was out of site) and listened to Rachel's answer. She answered very quietly. "It's not very nice to call someone that." And then she told her to keep playing the game.

I felt sick. I stayed in the bathroom for a very long time, and when I emerged, I said I wasn't feeling so well and wanted to walk back to Rachel's house. And so I did. Her mom was surprised when I walked over and left Rachel to babysit, but I said I'd had enough of the little girl and wanted to hang out with Rachel's sister.

"Oh, that little girl can be a handful, let me tell you!" Rachel's mom laughed down the hallway.

Rachel came home about an hour later and asked why I'd left. I'm not sure whether she ever knew what I'd heard, but I played it off like I was bored of babysitting. Shortly after that episode, she stopped babysitting for that little girl anyways—it wasn't really her thing.

Eighth grade was pretty uneventful. I had some friends in my classes and wasn't getting bullied quite as much, although there was still the occasional incident. It seemed that each time someone had a problem with me, the first words out of his or her mouth were, "you're so fat!"

An Asian girl in a few of my classes that year also happened to be in my gym class. During kickball one day, I accidently cut her in line without realizing it, and she asked me what I was doing. I said I didn't realize she was in line because she was sitting on a guardrail, talking to her friends, and not standing in line like the rest of us.

"She is such a fat ass—whatever. Trying to cut me in line—who the hell does she think she is?" I heard her say to her two other friends.

I ignored her and went about my day, but it was occurrences like that that made me stop and wonder whether I was really that fat. I asked my doctor to put me on a diet back in the sixth grade, but he wrote down raw carrots for an after-school snack, and that was enough to turn me off. I preferred eating half of the cookies in our jar with my dad after school, while he took a break from work and read the newspaper. We would both mindlessly read (cartoons for me, the news for him) and eat. Sometimes we devoured an entire loaf of soft, Italian bread, dipping it into the red sauce my mom had cooking on the stove for spaghetti and meatballs that night. Other times it was apple pie—we kept digging our forks into the pie until only crumbs were left.

I also became an expert at hiding wrappers. I was so sneaky that I could have had my own episode of *Law & Order*. While I never flushed them down the toilet (my parents would have beaten me silly if I'd destroyed our septic system), I got crafty at quietly munching in the kitchen, and the minute I heard footsteps or saw a car pull into the driveway, I threw the chips back into the cabinet as fast as I could and sped off to the living room sofa. By the time whoever was walking by saw me, it appeared as if I were just hanging out—you know, shooting the breeze. I also became a master of pushing candy wrappers to the bottom of the garbage can so no one could see them. Therefore, it was like I had never eaten the candy. I must have just woken up fat. I loved food and was obsessed with it. I would have taken a bullet for a bag of Cool Ranch Doritos.

You could say that I learned my bad eating habits from my family, although that sounds bad. My dad's side of the family is heavy, and my mom's side is relatively thin. My siblings always took after my mom's side, while it was obvious whose side I took after. There's a picture of my family and Poppy and Granny at an Italian restaurant on New Year's Eve of that year (2000—Y2K, when at the stroke of midnight we all thought the planet was going to explode and we would all be dead). In the picture, I'm sitting on one side of the table, next to my dad and Granny. On the other side is Mikey, Lin, my mom, and Poppy. Years later Lin came across the picture and said, "Oh look—all the heavy people are on one side of the table, and the skinny people are on the other!" In the picture I'm squeezing into a white Christmas sweater that was size PP (Pretty Plus, the big girls' section of the kids' department at Sears), and my cheeks are so rosy from all the blush I put on. I had on leggings before they were cool, and basically I looked like a squeezed sausage about to pork herself silly on brick-oven pizza.

The eighth-grade semiformal event was in June, and the boys started to ask the girls to be their dates. Sierra had a date, and so did most of the other girls I knew. I had no desire to go, and it wasn't until I was in the car with one of the girls on my softball team that it occurred to me that I should go. Her mom asked whether I had bought my dress yet, and I said, "I don't have a date; I wasn't planning on going." Her mom told me I should go and that not all the girls were going with dates.

My teammate next to me in the backseat had no date, and the dance fell on her birthday. I shrugged and decided I would go. Instead of buying a new dress, I borrowed a dress Kelly had worn for an event. It looked nice and had a matching shawl. Jo Jo came over, curled my hair, and put lip liner on me for the first time. I looked tan and felt pretty. My mom took me to get a manicure right after a softball game earlier in the week, and I had on shiny hoop earrings. I remember feeling pretty glam that night. The dance was great, and I had a really good time taking pictures of everyone and dancing. Middle school was over ... Hello, high school!

The summer before my freshman year was when my babysitting career took off. My mom mentioned to one of the moms in Lin's kindergarten class that I babysat for my younger cousins, and the mom immediately said she was looking for a babysitter for her daughter. She asked me to help her out the week before school started, and she picked me up outside our mailbox early in the morning and brought me back to her house, where I played with her daughter until around four o'clock in the afternoon, and then they drove me back home. She paid me great money, and I had a good time playing with Barbies and watching movies.

I was playing tennis on the high school team that fall, but once Halloween hit and tennis was over, I began to babysit for the little girl every day after school. My mom dropped me off, and I had a house key, so I let myself in. I walked their small dog and waited at the bus stop for the little girl to come home. I was only there for an hour and a half each day, but I made a snack, helped her with homework, and then played with her. She liked to eat junk food for her snack, and her mom always told me to help myself. S'mores, candy bars, and popcorn were her snacks of choice, and I easily gave in to temptation and ate some as well.

Then one day I realized I was tired of being fat. I had lost fifteen pounds in the spring of eighth grade from taking a kickboxing class once a week with my friend and eating a low-fat yogurt every day for lunch with my sandwich. Over the summer, however, the weight crept back on.

I gave up and continued to consume heavy meals with my family, and whenever I got a good grade on a test, my dad let me pick my favorite restaurant, and we went out to eat and celebrated on Saturday nights. I loved Chili's, so that's often where we went, occasionally switching it up with a Mexican and Chinese restaurant we liked. General Tso's chicken, an egg roll, and some spoonfuls of pork lo mein were my typical go-to at the Chinese place. At the Mexican place, I liked to load up on chips and salsa before the meal came out, and then I went to town on cheese enchiladas with refried beans. When we went out for Italian, I got the same thing as

Mikey—fettuccine Alfredo—and ate an entire bread basket myself, since the waiters often refilled it a few times.

"Oh sure, what the hell!" my dad said when the waiter asked us whether we wanted more bread. I had no concept of what eating healthy meant. Sure, I exercised when I played tennis, but until softball came in the spring, I didn't do much. And I ate too much to burn off anything and lose weight. I was close to two hundred pounds and not even fifteen years old yet.

Every diet out there—you name it, and I tried it. I tried eating low carb, but then I would miss candy and chips so much that I ate almost an entire box of crackers the first chance I got. I got so depressed about being overweight that I had suicidal thoughts. I grabbed my flab in the shower and cried out, "Why? I hate you!" I shook my belly fat so hard that I made temporary red marks. I also hated developing breasts in the fifth grade, but they say that happens to overweight teenagers; something with the hormones is different. That is also why I got my period during the first week of sixth grade, while friends didn't get theirs until they were fifteen. Being overweight speeds up your body, which is why I developed so young.

I had visions of cutting my fat off with a pair of scissors. I pinched my arm fat and walked awkwardly so my thighs didn't rub together, creating a red mark due to too much chaffing. I was so ashamed of my body and never wanted anyone to look at me, let alone hug or touch me. I was a monster, someone who never could fathom what it would be like to be thin and beautiful. My weight consumed me and was all I thought about. It was all others could think about as well, it seemed.

The summer before my sophomore year began, I sat with one of my tennis teammates on the courts after the rest of the team packed up to hit the locker room and then headed home. As we sat there in the August sun, the boy's soccer team was heading to the track to run laps. Most of them were shirtless, and a few caught my eye. I told her I thought one in particular was hot, and just after I told her that, I said, "But a guy like that would never go for a girl like me."

She looked at me and said, "You have such a pretty face; have you ever tried losing weight? You would be so pretty if only you lost some weight."

I never forgot that conversation or that day, but I did forget the girl, because I couldn't be friends with someone who talked to me like that.

I decided that during my sophomore year I was going to get thin, and I researched gastric bypass surgery and liposuction on the computer. Terrified of going under the knife, I quickly pushed those ideas out of my head. That is the easy way out, my doctor said. It takes a true person to do it the right way and stick with it through the ups and downs. Dieting and exercising aren't easy, but in the long run, will gastric bypass eliminate your muffin top? No.

I remember seeing Jenny Craig commercials and asking my mom whether I could join. We went to the meeting center one fall evening after tennis practice. The woman assigned to me measured my height and weight and then took my picture in the hallway. "Your 'before" picture! Honey, you're never going to see that number on the scale ever again!" she bellowed and then told us to follow her into her office. She shut the door and then asked me questions about my eating history and exercise habits. She asked whether being overweight was hereditary, and I looked over at my mom as she carefully chose her words.

"Yes, the members on my husband's side of the family are all overweight."

The woman then led me to a large walk-in freezer, and she literally went grocery shopping for me. I had a basket in my hand, and she threw in frozen meals. Then she walked me over to a pantry and threw in everything from Jenny Craig-brand tuna fish to granola bars. Except for fruits and vegetables, everything I consumed was supposed to be a Jenny Craig product. Since I was under eighteen, my mom signed the contract, paid, and we were off. I was apprehensive about eating Jenny Craig food all the time, though, especially because I had two sweet sixteen parties coming up. I mentioned this to the woman, and she said she would work with me to prepare for the party, and I could eat the foods there. But then she asked me whether this was going to be a "regular thing."

"You mean, like going out to eat?" I asked, and she nodded. I looked over at my mom, and we both said that our family liked to go out to eat every Saturday night, so once a week that would be an issue. Needless to say, I tried the Jenny Craig granola bar the next day in the bathroom in between classes and didn't enjoy it. The tuna was a weird color, and I wasn't allowed to add mayonnaise to it. Then, on top of all this, my dad read the entire

Jenny Craig contract and went through the roof when he realized the food was going to cost him about $400 a month.

"Let me get this straight—she has to eat only their food, and the rest of us have to suffer when she gets pissed off and can't have what were having?" Once he did the math and realized how much Jenny Craig food cost, it wasn't worth it. My mom three business days to terminate the contract and return all the food, and we did. I felt rather blue about Jenny Craig not working out when I read an article that resonated with me.

It was *People* magazine's annual "Half Their Size," and there was an article about a mother and daughter who'd together lost over 150 pounds by joining Weight Watchers. I knew nothing about Weight Watchers, and reading this article interested me. The teenage daughter and her mother were shown in their "before" picture while riding on horses, and they both looked humongous. They mentioned that they ate a lot of grilled chicken and brought their I Can't Believe It's Not Butter! spray with them to restaurants to give their plain chicken some taste. They looked so healthy and happy in their "after" picture that I begged my mom to take me to a meeting so I could see what Weight Watchers was all about. A week later, I stepped into a Weight Watchers meeting for the very first time.

The meeting center was held in a shopping center about fifteen minutes away and looked inviting. It was in a large white room with multiple chairs facing the front, and the leader stood and spoke to the audience after you weighed in at the scale. I was so afraid of everyone seeing my number on the scale, but no one actually saw it except the receptionist behind the desk, and she didn't shout it out or even tell me what it was; she wrote it down in my weigh-in log, and I read it myself when I got back to my chair.

The Thursday night meeting I went to was packed, and the leader talked about how she could eat anything she wanted to on Weight Watchers but in moderation. I had to measure out my food, and everything had a "point" value, so with the help of a tracking tool and a guidebook, I could figure out what to eat and what not to waste my daily points on. I was allowed a certain number of points a day, and when I went over that amount, I could dip into a weekly extra allowance; but when those extra points ran out, the party was over, and it was time to stop eating. The concept was intriguing to me, and we stayed after the meeting for an introductory session before my mom agreed to sign me up, and she paid the whole $120 up front for a ten-week package.

I got home and was so excited to start this new journey and finally be skinny. I wrote down, "135 lbs.—here I come!" at the top of my weekly food journal and left it out on the kitchen counter, where my dad saw it. "Oh, Tini, I don't know if you will ever be one hundred thirty-five pounds. Our bodies just aren't built that way. It's in our genes. It sucks, but we are built bigger." I looked at him and nodded because I knew he was right. I could lose some weight, but I never thought I could get to be very skinny, because our family truly wasn't built that way. "Short and stocky," we like to joke, but when it comes down to it, most of us are.

My first week on the program, I lost 4.4 pounds. Rachel was skeptical when I told her and said, "That's a lot of weight to lose the first week—our bodies aren't supposed to lose that much so soon."

I was over the moon. "It's water weight! They told us you lose more in the beginning!" I exclaimed, and by my third week there, I'd lost seven pounds.

One of my tennis teammates noticed the difference as we waited together for the bus. "I can tell you've lost weight!" she said, and I beamed from ear to ear. I was making better choices, but I had weeks when I slipped up. I had friends over after school, and they wanted chips and salsa. During those weeks I gained weight or didn't lose as much, but I was doing so well. Weight Watchers taught me how to measure my portions and make better food choices. My meeting was packed each week, and although there weren't too many people my age in the room, I found it inspiring to see people earn awards for their efforts.

I stayed with Weight Watchers all the way until the summer before college. I remember hitting numbers on the scale I never thought I would see and feeling ecstatic. I lost twenty-five pounds that summer, and even when my dad took us all to Disney World for a business trip/vacation, I came back and discovered I'd lost two pounds. We'd walked a lot in the theme parks, and I think my teenage metabolism helped. I also went to Cape May and Wildwood for a week with Chrissy and came back and lost weight. I remember swimming laps in the pool at the hotel and making good food choices. I did indulge, and I had a strawberry cheesecake/ice cream sundae one day and ice cream on other days, and loved every minute of it. But I was still eating better overall and walking a ton.

For brunch I always ordered my whole wheat toast "dry" and substituted egg whites in when I could. I became robotic, but it was a good thing; there was no need to stuff myself on pancakes, only to be hungry an hour later. Then summer went on, and it was time to leave my house and move into the dorms at my university. I spoke with my leader, and she mentioned there being a Weight Watchers center in my university's town; and when I called, someone said it was about an eight-minute drive from campus, but by no means was the trip walkable. The roads were curved and busy, so walking there would never have happened. So I had to say my good-byes and finish on my own.

And boy did I. After my family left and I was getting ready for school to start, I had tennis to keep me busy. I was working out for at least two hours a day when we had daily practice, and on the days we had matches, I had almost three hours of back-and-forth running around. I was eating ninety-calorie Special K granola bars as snacks, and I had my favorite (and now discontinued) Weight Watchers blueberry crunch cereal in the room. I poured some low-fat milk into a bowl, measured out a 3/4 cup of the cereal, and ate that while my hall mates pigged out on take-out pizza.

When we had movie nights in my room, I made low-fat popcorn and sprayed I Can't Believe It's Not Butter! on it. For breakfast I had my cereal with a banana or a packet of Quaker Weight Control Oatmeal in my room while my roommate slept. I carried a granola bar in my bag as something to nibble on in between classes, and then for lunch I went to either the cafeteria, where with one swipe the food was all I could eat or to our lovely sandwich shop in the academic building. The days I grabbed a sandwich were easy—I had turkey with mustard, lettuce, and tomato on a kaiser roll with a bag of Baked Lays or a soup, depending on what it was that day. On the days I went to the cafeteria, I had a healthy-sized portion of whatever was the specialty item of the day: tacos, pulled pork, chicken, and so forth. But I always stopped by the salad and fruit bar, and picked something out there also. For dinner I did the same thing, although some nights we finished with tennis so late that our cafeteria was closing, so only certain items were still out to grab. The deli section was always the last to be cleaned and closed for the night, so my teammates and I often made wrap sandwiches with side salads.

Needless to say, I was strict with my food and ate very well unlike, well, everyone around me. One night while my table full of girls went up for cookies and brownies for dessert, I went up to the fruit car, grabbed an apple and a scoop of peanut butter, and cut the apple with my butter knife. One of my friends remarked, "You're so proper! Here I am, looking like a slob, and you're cutting up your little apple and dunking it ever so slightly into the peanut butter!"

I treated myself to frozen yogurt almost every night after that and also had a Belgian waffle at times with whipped cream on top, or I picked up a bag of yogurt-covered pretzels from the pizza shop next to the cafeteria, and my roommate and I inhaled the bag in minutes. But I was working out with tennis so much that it didn't matter what I ate, although when I did eat, I made better choices than my peers.

When tennis came to an end around November, I started walking to the gym on campus. My dad had remarked on how nice and new the gym looked when we toured the school the year before; he said the paint job was fresh. The gym was a ten-minute walk, entirely uphill, from the dorms. I walked to that gym in rain or snow, sleet or slush, and my body thanked me for it. I mostly used the elliptical for an hour, but sometimes I mixed it up if it was taken and did the treadmill for an hour. I walked uphill, slowly building my incline as I went. I then used some of the circuit machines around the room and worked on strengthening my calves and arms. I asked the athletic director for a quick tutorial on how to use all the circuit machines, and he was happy to give me one.

On an especially crazy day, I went to the gym twice: once in the early afternoon and once after dinner. It was insane, but my roommate mentioned that she had done this once with another girl in our hallway when they were "feeling fat," so I thought I should too. I remember feeling so exhausted afterward and never did that ever again. I'm not sure how contestants on *The Biggest Loser* work out all day long like that; two hour-long workouts were enough to fatigue me. Now my roommate was a whole different story. She was 5'10 with long hair, and she was a former cheerleader, dating the former quarterback of their high school. Que the eye roll; c'mon, I know you want to. Her mom put pressure on her to be thin, and she was on the

Atkins diet when school first started and claimed it was what kept her thin and trim in high school.

"I was a fatty growing up!" she said. I stared at her and told her there was no way she was a former heifer. I was a former fatty, not her perfect self.

The one time she invited me to her house, her mom ran over to a picture in a frame and said, "Now, Katrina, are you ready for this? This is her in her fat days!" and burst into laughter while showing me the picture. My roommate looked geeky in a puffy sweater, but I wouldn't exactly call Jenny Craig for her. As we went up to her bedroom, she showed me a wicker basket on the floor, full of various bikinis in different prints and shapes.

"How many bathing suits do you own?" I asked. "You don't even own a pool!"

She said, "About twenty." I was floored; we had a beautiful in-ground pool, and I had three bathing suits I rotated wearing.

On another fall day, her mother came by to visit and asked whether I wanted to do lunch at Panera and hit T.J. Maxx. I was ecstatic to get off campus, and as I got out of their car to head into Panera, her mom said, "Katrina, look at you! You have lost a lot of weight since school started!" I was starting to look like a lean, mean fighting machine. A guy in one of my classes referred to me as "hot," and I was starting to really get my body to where I'd always wanted it to be.

I didn't have a lot of temptation around; I went to the pizza shop twice a week and got a grilled chicken sandwich or a slice of pizza, but I didn't get the fifteen mozzarella sticks like all my friends, nor did I get buffalo wings and cheese fries there in the wee hours of the morning. The pizza shop was the only place open late on campus, but it never intrigued me enough to order bad choices. I also frequented the coffee shop in our student center and got a fruit salad or panini, with an occasional brownie because they were just *that good*. Plus walking all over campus to get to class and meetings helped. Just as I was starting to reach my prime, my roommate started to hit her decline.

She started sneaking around with a guy on campus and was conveniently never around when her boyfriend called at night. She started to have late-night pancakes at the diner with that guy, and before long, she was wearing sweatpants all the time. She never looked fat; she was so tall and lean that her body just got thicker, and her face got rounder. However, she didn't seem too concerned. She was falling in love with the guy on campus, and before long, her high school sweetie was gone, and the new guy was her main squeeze. He showered her with heart-shaped treats, and she giggled while on the phone with him as she popped candies into her mouth from her freshly manicured hand.

Ironically she started buying clothes in size 8, which was the size I was just beginning to introduce myself to. I'd always hovered around a 12 to 14 (although one jean dress from Old Navy was a size 18, and I will never forget seeing that number on a tag), so being anything below a 10 was inconceivable to me. My mom took me shopping in the early winter and paid for a new wardrobe for me, as a thin person waiting to bust out. I got a nice pair of beige high-heeled boots, some tight tank tops and sweaters, and a pair of pants. I didn't go crazy but felt like a brand-new person in my new designer duds.

My roommate, on the other hand, had a mother who wasn't exactly supportive of her new size. Her mother began sending her packages consisting of Weight Watchers starting kits, which she wrote in her note that she bought off eBay; they were so heavily discounted that they were "basically free." My roommate and I laughed ourselves silly when these packages arrived, and it soon became obvious that the only person who had an issue with a recent weight gain was the person not carrying the weight, as is the case in most scenarios.

That November 2005 I reached my lowest weight ever, down forty pounds in total. On the day the scale read 138, I was over the moon and couldn't believe my eyes. I, of course, still wanted to lose three more pounds to get down to 135 and be at the number I'd always dreamed about, the same one my dad had said was unachievable for someone in our family. I never did get down to 135 but hovered around 140 to 145 all throughout college, which was fine, and I was still incredibly toned.

It was during that Thanksgiving weekend when I was home that my family took notice of my shrunken size. As I was heading down the steps into our basement, Mikey said, "Whoa, man! Look at you!" which was the only compliment capable of a high school sophomore. My dad took notice of this and came around the corner, asking whether I had been eating all the meals I was allocated per week in the cafeteria, and I said that yes, of course, I was. He turned to my mom and said, "She is doing this to spite me. I just know it. Pissing away my money when she is not even eating on campus." He yelled down the staircase to me that Karen Carpenter wasn't someone to be admired.

And then it began to happen. Everywhere I seemed to go back home, people took notice of my forty-pound weight loss. My old coworkers at the bagel shop were in awe of me, and one didn't even recognize me. Old friends from high school came into the bagel shop while I was working over winter break and squealed when they saw me turn around behind the counter, wearing a much smaller white apron. I no longer craved bagel sandwiches and Sicilian slices of pizza and the greasy food I used to consume at restaurants with my friends.

And just like I was taught at Weight Watchers, not everyone will support your new lifestyle. Some didn't know how to handle this; they tried to push fatty and sugary foods my way and made statements like "Oh, come on—you're skinny enough. Just have one!" But we are taught in those weekly meetings that no one ever got the way he or she was from just "one" of anything. "One" became "twenty-one" very quickly. Trust me, I was a closet binger for a while. Although I never vomited, (I tried it once, but it didn't work...typical story of my life) I did try to starve myself during my junior year of high school, but that backfired when I regained my appetite and went hog wild. I've never understood people who eat just one cookie or slice of pizza.

Jillian Michaels once said that we need to stop equating emotions with food. That's hard to do, because I love food and everything about it. While some members of my family ate to live, I was always on the side of the family who lived to eat. I love the way chips crunch in my mouth or a soft brownie melts in my mouth. However, I try not to abuse food anymore, but it is a day-to-day challenge.

That spring I was rocking a new black tank top, when a few of my friends in the hallway thought we should all be silly and take sexy pictures. In my few shots, I'm straddling a chair and posing seductively. They did my eyes all smoky, and my hair was big and curly, and I wore some tight jeans; I looked as good as Britney Spears in her heyday. I sometimes look at those shots and chuckle, but I'm mostly proud of how hard I worked to look that good. When I went out to a restaurant, I ordered a chicken Caesar salad with no croutons and the dressing on the side or a hamburger with no mayonnaise or French fries. And you know what? I never missed the French fries or croutons.

After a while, I sounded robotic ordering like that, and friends and family made fun of me, but I was determined to be thin and stay thin. According to my doctor's chart, I could have lost another twenty pounds, and then I would have been in the healthy range for a girl my age. I also would have looked like a skeleton and been starving all the time. Some people want to lose a ton of weight and rock those size-two jeans, but that was never my intention. I never thought I would see the day that I wore a size 10, let alone a size 6 or 8! I was on cloud nine.

As freshman year ended, my mom and I went outlet shopping for the first time, and I picked out some really cute clothes. I was finally rocking clothes from the cool stores—she even bought me a hoodie from Abercrombie & Fitch.

That summer Jo Jo was eating really healthily, and I went over to her condo for dinner in between my summer classes. I had one class in the morning and one in the evening, but instead of going home in between, I worked out and then showered and ate dinner at her place, since she was only a quick ride from campus. She made us veggie burgers with couscous and a side of chutney. I had gained back five pounds but was still down thirty-five, so I saw no reason to worry. I still looked good, right? Well, the answer to that question was yes, but I still should have watched it. Because by the time my sophomore year, winter semester, rolled around, I was up fifteen pounds.

The weight had snuck up so quickly. I was still working out daily and had tennis in the fall, don't forget. Yet you can work out for hours and still gain weight—it all depends on how much food and what food you are consuming. Suddenly, you allow yourself to start eating some french fries with that hamburger, and instead of a salad for lunch, you want a wrap sandwich. Then you do it again because you remember how good it tasted. Then before long, you are sneaking cookies from the jars of the babysitting houses while the kids are tucked in their beds and Mommy and Daddy aren't due home for another four hours. Some days you call your neighbor back home while you both are babysitting, and you giggle over which house has the "better" pantry. You note her advice to make sure you "even out the top of the ice cream with a spoon so the families don't know how much you really ate," and you tell yourself it will never get to that point, but it almost always does. The parents are wealthy and generous, and they always tell you to treat their home like it is yours and help yourself to anything and everything in their kitchen. So I did.

I babysat once to twice a week, so the pantries were fully stocked each time I went. I knew which houses ate only organic, which ones had the most junk food, and which had no food at all for me to mindlessly consume. My mom kept telling me to stop eating their food, but they always told me to help myself, and although I wouldn't consider myself a thrill seeker, there was something awfully exciting about sneaking someone else's food. That gave me the rush I so desperately sought. Instead of feeling the thrill of getting ready for a big date and making small talk with a tall, dark-haired stranger in a dimly lit restaurant, I got the rush I needed in a dimly lit pantry belonging to people I didn't even know.

Quicker that I thought, I gained a few more pounds and was feeling pretty blue one night as I was studying in my dorm, when I heard a knock on my door. It was my suitemate, and she wanted to borrow a plastic spoon. I answered the door with a jar of chunky peanut butter in one hand and a metal spoon in the other. I told her I would check my drawer for a plastic spoon.

"Katrina, you complain that you're gaining weight, and here you are, eating peanut butter straight out of the jar with a spoon!" she cried, her eyes wide and bewildered as if she'd just caught me snorting cocaine. "Put that away! Stop it!" she said, and I did, realizing maybe she had a point. She was also the same suitemate who told me I looked so much better with makeup on because if "only I spent more time on myself in the mornings, maybe I would get a boyfriend." As I put the lid back on my peanut butter, I told myself I had a problem.

Not long before that party with the peanut butter, I went to a gathering in the dorm of one of my Campus Crusade for Christ friends. Yes, that was one of the *many* clubs I was in at college. It was in that dorm that one of the snacks happened to be Hershey's Kisses, a confection I don't even love that much and wouldn't even consider one of my favorites. The bowl was placed near my feet, and as we all sat around the room, watching a movie, we munched. I ate the kisses, since they were the closest thing to me. Well, by the time the movie ended and someone turned the lights on, the girl next to me felt the need to say, "Oh my God! You ate so many Kisses! Look at your pile of wrappers!" I wanted to jump out the third-floor window at that moment. Who says something like that? Aloud? At a Campus Crusade for Christ movie night?

Before my weight spun more out of control, I knew I needed to join Weight Watchers again. I asked my future junior-year roommate whether she would take me to the meetings every Wednesday. She was the only person I was friendly with who had her car on campus and didn't work on Wednesdays, when most of the campus was off from class. She explained that her mom used to be on Weight Watchers and had lost a ton of weight on it, so she understood my embarrassment when I asked her to drive me to the meetings. We made it our routine; she would sit by my side at the meetings, encourage good behaviors during the week, and hit the gym with me often. It was a struggle, but by the time summer arrived, I was down twenty pounds and feeling pretty fantastic again.

For me, losing weight while living in the dorms wasn't the hardest goal on the planet; I had access to a free gym that was not only clean but also had state-of-the-art equipment. I had seen a lot worse in other gyms, so this one suited my needs just fine. I also started taking kickboxing once a week in the dance studio in our recreation center. Going home was where the problems always began.

My mom is a great cook, and while she does take the time to make me some Weight Watchers-friendly foods, not everything she makes is like that. My family doesn't like ground turkey meat and instead prefers the full-fat beef dripping with grease. The same goes for pork, so you can imagine how Sunday night spaghetti dinner goes with meatballs, sausage, pasta, salad, and homemade garlic bread. And dessert afterward could be anything from a full-fat brownie (not the kind I make with plain Greek yogurt) to cookies or fresh doughnuts from the Italian bakery in town. All this probably has your mouth watering, but to someone who has literally spent half of their life on Weight Watchers, you might as well just shoot me now.

All those items are more than an entire day's worth of my Weight Watchers points, so sure I can eat all that, but that's all I can consume for the entire day, and I may need to skip breakfast tomorrow. So you see that that just isn't a feasible way for me to live. It frustrates me when I see my friends gobble those items up and stay skinny when I know for a fact that if I gobble anything up, I will see a weight gain on the scale the following week.

"Is my metabolism dead?" I asked my doctor once during a checkup. He chuckled and said no, but it just may be "very slow." Fantastic. He encouraged me to drink two cups of green tea a day and also mentioned that my cholesterol is fantastic and so is my body fat index, so clearly my workouts and consumption of lean meats and low fat dairy are working. I have seen my body go up and down in size, but when I'm eating clean and hitting my workout classes hard each night after work, I feel my best. I look toned, my bras fit better, without back fat bunching in places where it shouldn't be; even my chest gets a natural lift.

Of course, I sometimes visit the "old neighborhood," like my one Weight Watchers leader once said. But I cannot stay there—meaning that I may go to Chili's and order some of the food I used to eat in high school, the food that got me into this mess in the first place, but then hours later, I may feel physically sick. The sodium and fat content literally set my body into overdrive, and I spend most of the evening in the bathroom. I cannot handle such fatty foods in my system anymore, and this fact makes me sad, because I love the way those foods look and smell—and, of course, taste—but the end result isn't pretty. I still have trouble learning my lesson and will eat certain old trigger foods, but then I eat my one piece and move on. I don't eat the entire block of cheddar cheese like I used to, nor do I consume twenty mini hot dogs anymore.

I truly feel sorry for myself sometimes; I'm sorry I cannot eat what I want and sorry that food controls me so much. A slice of pizza or a bag of Oreos shouldn't be my worst enemy, but they are. As I was taught at my weekly meetings, out of sight, out of mind. If it isn't there, you won't grab it. That is the case now that I own my own home and live alone; if I don't bring the junk home, it has no way of getting there. And I don't.

I was craving "real" ice cream last week and had none in my freezer, so I walked over to the local ice cream shop in my neighborhood and bought myself a kiddie cup of cake-batter ice cream and enjoyed every morsel of it. I could have easily bought an entire tub of ice cream for three dollars at the grocery store, but what good would that have done me? No one ever has *one* small bowl of ice cream and goes about his or her day. He or she keeps dipping into it until half the container is gone, and then he or she feels so crappy that he or she runs over to the sink, rinses the remainder out with hot water, and throws out the evidence, asking himself or herself why on earth a three-dollar tub of rocky road ice cream has just ruined his or her entire evening.

So to that I say, "No, thank you." The same goes for baked goods. If I'm really craving a doughnut or cookie, I go out and buy one. For a soft, gooey one from a bakery, I may pay three dollars, while I can buy an entire box at the grocery store for three dollars, but that quantity is dangerous for me. Plus bakeries and ice cream shops make fresh and delicious treats, so spending three dollars and really enjoying it is better than buying any old item sitting on a shelf or in a freezer. "A moment on the lips, a lifetime on the hips!" they always told us at meetings.

While it may seem I'm getting my life on track, working out five days a week, cooking lean, and always counting my Weight Watchers points, I'm not always perfect. I have days I slip up and eat like a beast at a party, but then I think back to my leaders who told us not to let a bad day turn into a bad week. Before I was on Weight Watchers, if I had a bad day with food choices, I just shrugged and said, "The hell with it!" My dad would tell me the tendency to be overweight was in our genes; no matter how much I tried, I was never destined to be thin.

I'm still not *that* thin compared to the average girl my height, but that's fine. I know what number on the scale feels best to me and how good wearing a size 6 or 8 feels compared to the days I was squeezing into a size 14. I look in the mirror and see someone who is constantly told on Facebook how pretty I am in my profile pictures and someone my cousins always refer to as their "younger cousin who loves to work out." I no longer have so much belly fat that I grab it in the bathroom, nor do I cry in the shower over how jiggly my arm fat is or how I was one of the first girls in my grade to develop breasts. My body is actually quite toned these days from years of daily workouts.

I have much more confidence than I did while growing up, and I owe Weight Watchers a big thank-you for changing my life. I speak up at my Weight Watchers meetings and give suggestions to struggling members. I smile at strangers when I walk my six miles every Saturday in my neighborhood. I talk to people when I travel, those whom I normally wouldn't talk to; losing weight has changed my ability to speak and use my voice. When I was carrying an extra fifty pounds on my body, I never dared to speak, because I was always bullied. Once you have heard, "Well, who asked you anyway, fat ass?" you know never to argue back with a bully and instead just go about your way, walking as fast as you can, telling yourself everything will be all right.

I had some good memories on the scale and some bad ones over the years, but I knew what I had to do to keep going. I know what items I need stocked in my refrigerator at all times to feel confident in my meal choices. I have *never* looked in the fridge and found nothing to eat, so I "just had to" call and order a large pizza. That has never happened and never will. My mind doesn't necessarily think about those items anymore. Yes, on some days all I do is think about food and how excited I am for my next meal. I could be showering and thinking about making a bag of popcorn for the movie I'm about to watch or doing plank push-ups in boot camp and fantasizing about how much I would love a slice of sausage pizza from Pizza Hut.

But I snap out of that thinking really fast. Pizza is delicious, but I like to make it myself where I can add low-skim cheese, fresh vegetables, and turkey pepperoni. It comes out looking and tasting damn good, and I don't feel disgusting after I eat it.

I now pass my yearly physical with flying colors, and my doctor is always quite impressed with my cholesterol and lean eating habits. I love to exercise and really feel and look better when I do it. Dripping with sweat after a workout puts me in the happiest frame of mind, and I truly feel the sexiest in gym clothes, grabbing onto the elliptical machine at my local YMCA, not in a tight dress with huge heels and with so much makeup on that my skin cannot breathe. That's not the real me.

I know years have passed since anyone called me a "pig," but I will admit that when I'm in a mall or movie theater and walk past a group of teenagers and hear them telling a story and the words *fat* or *fat ass* is used, I get red in the face and walk as fast as I can. I tell myself they are just talking about someone they know at school, not me. But I do find myself getting sweaty, and my pulse races. I get the same feeling when my cousins tell stories about all the times I grabbed food off their plates during Sunday night dinners; we all get a good chuckle out of it, but deep down, I want to strangle someone. Lastly, one day I want my children to know how wonderful life can be and that although adolescence can be terrible, life does get better. Although people may choose to treat you like you are nothing, that doesn't mean you *are* nothing.

Life is short, and we need to get out there and live. I wasn't living when I was so overweight that I had trouble running one lap around the track because I was winded. I also wasn't truly living each time I tried on a prom dress and needed help getting out of it, because I had squeezed myself into it so much that I almost ripped it.

Nowadays, I really enjoy my "me" time. I'm a happy homeowner who meets friends basically wherever I go, due to my outgoing personality. I have a few workout buddies who push me to go further and tell me I can keep going when I want to stop. The day I ran my first 5K and didn't keel over and die was nothing short of a victory for me, and the same went for my first fourteen-mile bike ride. It would have been physically impossible for me not only to enjoy these activities years ago but also to go places on my own and meet friends who also enjoy similar activities. My former couch-potato self is so far gone that I wouldn't be able to find her if I tried.

Every June on my birthday, I treat myself to a McDonald's Big Mac with medium French fries, and I'm truly the happiest person alive. I indulge with a cupcake that night with my family and am able to honestly enjoy my night. Years of practice got me to where I am today, and I'm still not perfect, but I'm eating a hell of a lot better than the old me. No one wants to spend his or her life starving. I just make smarter choices in life, in love, and with my lasagna these days.

CPSIA information can be obtained
at www.ICGtesting.com
Printed in the USA
LVOW11s1751200717
542032LV00002B/437/P